GO
FORWARD

MOVING *FORWARD*
AS A GENERATION
WHOLLY FOR CHRIST

Scott DeGroff

Go Forward – Moving Forward as a Generation Wholly for Christ
By Scott DeGroff
Copyright © 2021

Published by Warren A. Henderson Publishing
1025 Iron Cap Drive
Stevensville, MT 59870

Cover Design by Benjamin Bredeweg

Perfect Bound ISBN: 978-1-939770-64-6
eBook ISBN: 978-1-939770-65-3

Copies of *Go Forward* are available through various online retailers worldwide.

Foreword

It is said that ninety percent of finding the solution to a problem is understanding the problem. In this book Scott DeGroff identifies some very real issues in our western Christianity (and possibly the world over) — We have all too often traded the one true God with idols made in the image of our very own desires, wills, occupations, abilities, and dreams.

Scott bears his soul to those who are willing to consider the reality of our great need and wake up from what has become all too acceptable. His powerful reflections on **purity** in our lives, **prayer** as essential, **passion** for God's passions, **power** for radical living and **pursuit** of the lost have led me to deep introspection. It's there that I too have recognized the black & white contrast of the ugliness of my heart when compared with the heart of God. But, as is always true about God, He wounds to heal. Each of the short chapters are filled with truth and testimony of God's power to change those who are willing to respond to His call for us to leave all and follow Him. It is there that we will find that the gods we have made were not gods at all and that "in Him we live, move and have our being" (Acts 17:28a).

May you be challenged and moved by the words that follow.

— Rich Brown (Int'l Ministries
Ethnos360/Global Partners)

Team Endorsements

As a friend and ministry partner, it has been an absolute delight to watch Scott passionately pursue the Lord Jesus Christ daily. His fierce desire to encourage sleeping saints to wake up and wholeheartedly run the race is evident to all who know him. In this concise and sincere book, he beautifully communicates the path forward for God's people.

— Dan Williams

Over the past few years, my friendship with Scott has grown through seeking the Lord together in prayer. Today, I am blessed to call him not only a dear friend but also a valued teammate in the Lord's work in California. Scott loves being in the Lord's presence and the love of God flows from his life. What he shares in Go Forward expresses the beauty of what God can do in a life completely yielded to Him. My encouragement would be to prayerfully read each chapter, expecting God to also work in your life!

— Micah Williams

Table of Contents

Dedication

Dedicated to Jesus Christ the Savior of the world and the most amazing Person any of us will ever meet.

You, Lord Jesus are more delightful, more of a Friend, a better and more present Teacher, a more gentle Shepherd, and more perfect Guide than I ever thought could be enjoyed in this life. It blows my mind every day that I have a real, tangible, daily relationship with You.

Hebrews 11:4c says of the faith of Abel that You commended *"him by accepting his gifts."* I offer this book to You as an offering. If, someday, eternity shows that You accept it and are pleased and glorified, then, whatever else may or may not come of it will be inconsequential.

I love You, Lord. To know You is to love You and to know You better is to love You with an all-consuming, passionate, focused love. You are the Exceedingly Great Reward.

Please take this little book and do with it what You please. It is my gift of love to You.

— Scott DeGroff

Preface

The intent of this little book is to express a deep burden the Lord has given. If you are sincerely longing for Christ, or if you are willing to let the Lord work in you so that you are longing for Christ, then this is for you!

This book is intended to move us forward on a journey with the Lord, the end result being a yielded people more in love, more filled, more free, and more excited than ever to walk each day with the Savior and to watch Him win in our generation.

*"Give us help from trouble, for the help of man is useless. Through God we will **do valiantly**."* Psalm 60:11-12a

*"And the Lord said to Moses, 'Why do you cry to Me? Tell the children of Israel to **go forward**!'"* Exodus 14:15

The Lord Moved In Me

I was in Ontario, Canada, speaking at a Bible conference. Upon finishing the weekend, I got back into my rental car and headed across the border to New York, where I was to catch a plane in Buffalo for the rest of my trip home. As I crossed the border and turned on my phone, I heard a string of beeps and buzzes as the messages I had missed while out of the country started pouring in. I waited to catch up on all of it until I had returned my car in Buffalo, taken a shuttle to the airport, checked in for my flight, and finally gone through security. Then, my phone rang. On the line was one of the elders in my home church letting me know that the speaker for our upcoming weekend conference was unable to come. This conference was to be held in four days, and he asked me to pray about the possibility of taking all five sessions. I told him that I was happy to pray about it, and after a brief chat, we ended the conversation, and I boarded my plane for Atlanta.

When the airplane touched down in Atlanta, I again turned on my phone. During my brief layover it rang one more time – my elders were now officially asking me if I would speak at the weekend conference. I had prayed about it on the way from Buffalo to Atlanta, and told them I was at peace about it, would be happy to accept, and that I would ask the Lord what He would have me to say over the coming weekend.

When I boarded the next plane, this time headed to Kansas City, I began to ask the Lord, with my open Bible in front of me, what He wanted to say to His people during the upcoming

1

conference. Wondering and praying about that question led me to looking out my window at the millions of people we were flying over, and I became almost overwhelmingly burdened by the weight of the souls underneath us. There are over 325 million souls in the United States of America and over 35 million souls in Canada. With approximately 215 million in the rest of North America, that brings us to a total somewhere around 575 million souls that are deeply loved of Jesus Christ.

Never before in my life had I felt a burden like this, almost smothering me with its weight. I asked the Lord over and over again, "How are we going to reach them? What is it going to take for the people of God to move forward in the work You have clearly instructed us to do? What is wrong that we are not seeing the work move as we long for it to?"

As I sat before the Lord, reading a bit, but mostly praying and looking out my window, the Lord impressed on my heart the following word,

"Purity"

Then, I cried. I did my best to hide it, looking out the window and away from the crowded plane. I cried because I'm part of the Bride of Christ on this continent that is cheating on the Bridegroom. I cried because we are not a pure people. I cried because of my own failures and the failures of the Bride of Christ of which I'm a part.

I wrote down the word *"purity"* on a used note card in my Bible and I sat, embarrassed, while I wept before the Lord. (Please, let me say here that this is very unusual for me. I cry some during messages from a pulpit, but to sit on a plane weeping, my shoulders shaking – this was embarrassing to me.) I sat there thinking, "The people around me must think I'm crazy. They must be thinking, Who is this religious nut with his Bible open on his tray table, crying?" But, nonetheless, I sat there and wept before the Living God.

After some time of prayer and confessing my own sins and the sins of the spiritual family of which I am so privileged to be a part, I again asked the Lord, "What must be true for the Bride of Christ in North America to move forward?" The Lord, after some time of waiting before Him, impressed on my heart:

"Prayer"

Then, I cried again. I cried because we are not a people of prayer. I cried because the prayer meetings in North America are largely gone, or so feeble that there is no attraction to the Christians. I cried because I am a part of groups of Christians that see corporate prayer in the Word of God and hold up the value of disciplined labor in prayer, personal and corporate, and yet the prayer meeting is the least attended meeting of probably 97% of the local churches that I have the privilege of visiting - and that is in the circles of the body of Christ that still think it even worthwhile to have weekly corporate prayer meetings. A huge part of the body of Christ in this land doesn't have meetings for corporate prayer anymore. Vast percentages of the body of Christ aren't spending any significant time in prayer at all. If your body stops talking to your head, you are in HUGE trouble. I cried because, to an extent that only our Great and Awesome God knows, that is where we are – the body (the Church) doesn't see the desperate need to be talking to the Head.

3

I wrote the word *"prayer"* on my little note card, wept before the Lord, and continued asking the Lord for what must be true for us to move forward with Him and for Him. And then came word number three, impressed on my heart by the Lord:

"Passionate"

And there I sat and wept before the Lord because the Bride of Christ in this land is at least, and may I please emphasize, AT LEAST, as fascinated by football and many other things as we are about our relationship with Jesus Christ. Please don't get me wrong, I have nothing against football. I played it and loved it. I purchased and watched the Super Bowl on iTunes the day after the game because I was traveling home from a conference during the game. I pray especially for Christ-honoring athletes to stay strong and to honor the Lord in all they say and do, and I thank the Lord for the platform the Lord has given them to proclaim Christ! All this is to say that I'm not preaching against events or activities. I sat there weeping, not because these things exist or because we like them. I sat there weeping because we are much more passionate about these things than we are about knowing Him, loving Him, speaking of Him, spending time with Him, and ordering our lives in such a way that when every Christian stands before Him at the Judgment Seat of Christ, we can give an account with joy to the One who *"loved us and gave Himself up for us."* (Ephesians 5:2b) I sat there weeping not because we are not a passionate people, but because our passions are rooted in the wrong places.

Down on my note card went word number three, and I continued on my journey with the Lord. Again, after a bit of time the Lord impressed on my heart:

"Power"

By this time, I was a bit dried up of tears, (praise the Lord!) and I just sat there, feeling like I had just been through the funeral of a deeply loved relative. I was emotionally spent and exhausted from the past weekend of speaking and also from what the Lord was impressing on me now. I sat there thinking of the power of God that is evident in biblical history. I thought of the power of the Living God that is testified to so beautifully in missionary biographies. I thought of the power of our El Elyon (Most High God) that has been recorded during and after the hundreds of revivals throughout our Church age.

I sat wondering if power like that is available in our day. I sat pondering all the Lord has chosen to tell us about power in His Word, and I prayed that the Lord would teach me and open His Word to me, as I sought to rightly divide His mind on this subject in the coming days and weeks.

I wrote down word number four, *"power,"* and looked out the window. Thinking to myself I said, "We must be pure. We must be prayerful. We must be passionate." An outline was coming together. "We must have power" – His power in and through us. Then I sat quietly before the Lord wondering what else was needed.

Finally came the fifth and final word the Lord would impress on my heart and mind.

"Pursue"

We must pursue. We must go after the lost the way that Jesus Christ did. We must feel about them the way He feels about them. We must think about them the way He thinks about them and then act toward them the way He would have us to act toward them. A preacher stood in our pulpit a number of years ago and with tears coming down his face said, "I think we are not out there telling them about Jesus Christ because we love ourselves more than we love them!"

I repented that day. Many of us did. We repented of falling short. We repented of wrong priorities. We repented of loving things that don't matter in eternity and not loving things that do. I will never forget the spontaneous prayer meeting that followed the Lord's message to us that day. We asked the Lord to move amongst us and change us. It was the first step on a journey that we are still joyfully taking with and for the Living God.

I must confess that when the Lord impressed this final thought on my mind and heart, I again wept before Him. I wept this time realizing in some small way the price that had been paid for precious eternal souls and the longing that Jesus Christ feels to have them reconciled to Himself through believing the gospel and being saved. I wept thinking of an entire generation of 575 million souls in North America that we have been instructed to go and make disciples of for Jesus Christ. I wept, again in some small way, as Jesus Christ wept in Luke 19, wanting the blessing of precious souls but knowing that they are headed toward judgment. I wept over what makes Jesus Christ weep.

So, my friend, this is where the guts of this little book came from. I am earnestly and daily praying for the reaching of North America in this generation. I read my Bible and I find some generations that obeyed the Lord and followed His Word, but I find more generations that refused the blessing of obedience to the Living God and lived fruitless lives because of it. I long to be a part of a generation in North America that obeys the Lord and seeks after Him with a pure and focused, devoted love.

Dear fellow Christian, will you take this journey with me? Will you lay your life before a worthy Lord and Savior and ask for such conformity to the Word of God in your life that many will think it radical or perhaps call it revival? Will you be like the followers of God in Ezra's day who came before the Lord, *"to seek from Him the right way for us and our little ones and all our possessions?"* (Ezra 8:21b) They laid out everything before the Lord looking to Him for His BEST in their lives. You have to love the attitude of that verse! It is as if they are saying, "Here we are Lord; You say the word and Your people who love You will do it! If You want something from me, please say it Lord! If You want something different in my kids' lives, let me know and give me grace to implement it. If You want any or all of my possessions, please say the word and show me what to do!" Can you imagine a Bride of Christ in this land with such an attitude?!? May the Lord move among the body of Christians in North America to revive for Himself a Bride who has such a focus! I want to be part of a Bride on this continent that really loves Jesus Christ and is wholly sold out for Him!

If you are willing, please, (while on your knees or on your face if possible), commit this to the Lord in prayer and let's expectantly walk through this and see what the Lord will show us. Never forget, the Living God will take you seriously and take you at your word.

"So we fasted and entreated our God for this, and He answered our prayer." Ezra 8:23

Can we be casual in the work of God – casual when the house is on fire, and people in danger of being burned?

— Duncan Campbell

We Must Be Pure

"Now the purpose of the commandment is love from a pure heart." 1 Timothy 1:5a

PURE: Not mixed or adulterated with any other substance or material, innocent or morally good.

God Is Pure

Jesus Christ is God. Jesus Christ is God in the flesh. Jesus Christ is perfectly, spotlessly, beautifully pure. The theme of the Purity of God runs like a beautiful ribbon through His Word:

"You are of purer eyes than to behold evil, and cannot look on wickedness." Habakkuk 1:13

"The words of the Lord are pure words." Psalm 12:6

"The commandment of the Lord is pure." Psalm 19:8b

"God is light and in Him is no darkness at all." 1 John 1:5b

We desperately need a fresh sense of the infinite purity of our amazing God! If we could get a fresh sense of the purity of Jesus Christ, of what it was like for a spotless Lamb

> *of God to be identified with sin on a sinner's*
> *cross, of how disgusting sin is to Him and*
> *what it caused Him to suffer, it would*
> *radically change our lives and habits.*

Just how seriously does God take the purity of His people? As we read through our Old Testament scriptures, we find both one-time cleansings of the children of Israel (a rich picture for us of the washing and renewal of salvation; Titus 3:5b).We also find that it is not enough for a child of God to be cleansed one time and then to walk on through life anyway he sees fit. Instead we see that every time one of God's servants approaches Him, that servant must approach in a pure way. The Lord gives a great picture for this in the laver of the tabernacle where He says that when His servants approach Him, they must wash their hands and feet, "LEST THEY DIE". And then He repeats it in the passage, *"So they shall wash their hands and their feet, LEST THEY DIE"* (Exodus 30:17-21 emphasis mine).

It seems a fair question to ask, "Is the biblical God a bloodthirsty God?" or, "Is the God of the Bible like a selfish Greek god, standing on a cloud with a thunderbolt in his hand ready to let loose if anyone steps out of line, or if he just has a bad day?" The answer to that is categorically, "NO!" The God of the Old Testament is the God of the New, and He has always been a God of love and grace.

"The Lord is merciful and gracious, slow to anger, and abounding in mercy." Psalm 103:8

"Therefore the LORD will wait, that He may be gracious to you; ...that He may have mercy on you." Isaiah 30:18a

So, why does this gracious and merciful God say twice that if His servants don't approach Him having washed they will die? He is communicating His heart to show how seriously He takes the purity of His people! He is telling His people, *"You must be pure,"* not just positionally or initially (through salvation made pure before God), but in a practical ongoing way as you walk through this life (practical holiness and a lifestyle of purity)!

In my mind I hear some well-intentioned Christians say, "That is a very Old Testament sounding teaching and I see that you are referring to OT scriptures to make your point. I serve a New Testament God and I don't think my NT God would take such a strong or harsh stance."

Please, my friend, on behalf of Jesus Christ, take the time to look intently at God's New Testament heart in 1 Corinthians 11:29-30. In the context of a uniquely NT event, the Lord's Supper, the same biblical God says a remarkably similar thing! *"For he who eats and drinks in an unworthy manner eats and drinks judgment to himself, not discerning the Lord's body. For this reason many are weak and sick among you, and many sleep."* Please notice first that if they approach the Lord (or if anyone else in the Church Age approaches the Lord) in a manner that is unworthy, the Lord says they are eating and drinking judgment to themselves. And then, please notice the consequences! *"Many are weak and sick among you, and many sleep."* In other words, some were suffering physical sicknesses because of their lack of pure obedience to God's command, and others had been taken home to heaven where they would no longer grieve the heart of God through their improper walk before Him!

The biblical God takes purity more seriously than we are capable of comprehending. May the Spirit of God take these biblical truths and so sear them on our hearts and minds that we will be radically changed to be the pure Bride that Christ

11

deserves! Jesus Christ was, is, and ever will be, perfectly, spotlessly, beautifully pure! May we have eyes to see Him for Who and What He is!

We Must Be Pure

The current state of purity (or lack of purity, in my observation) among the people of God in our land is deeply grievous. I don't mean any criticism by it. In fact, I find myself more reluctant than ever to say anything negative about God's dear people, yet I don't know how else to say it. I find myself feeling as is described in 2 Corinthians 11:2, *"For I am jealous for you with godly jealousy."* I am jealous for Jesus Christ to receive the affection, devotion, and attention that He deserves, and I am jealous for the One who stands at the door and knocks, yet finds so few who are willing to open and enjoy intimacy with Him. Sadly, this has all too often been the case in my own Christian life.

So, the apostle Paul says in 2 Corinthians that he is jealous on behalf of Jesus Christ. Well, there is someone infinitely more important than Paul, who feels the same way. James 4:5b says, *"The Spirit who dwells in us yearns jealously."* Wow, the Spirit of God is jealous! Exodus 34:14 brings out a similar thought when it says, *"For you shall worship no other god, for the Lord, whose name is Jealous, is a jealous God."* The apostle Paul was jealous on behalf of Christ, the Spirit of God is jealous on behalf of Jesus Christ, and God Himself is a jealous God who deserves the focused love of His people. This idea is so striking, yet it makes perfect sense when you think it through. This God deserves the focused love of His people.

The Lord has always chosen to reveal His intended relationship with us through the picture of a marriage. In the Old Testament, the Lord wed Himself to the nation of Israel and even wrote out a certificate of divorce at one point.

*"For your Maker is your husband, The L*ORD *of hosts is His name; And your Redeemer is the Holy One of Israel; He is called the God of the whole earth."* Isaiah 54:5

"I had put her away and given her a certificate of divorce." Jeremiah 3:8b

The followers of God in Old Testament times were often not faithful to Him, and in Jeremiah 13 and 14 the unfaithfulness of the Lord's people caused the Omnipotent Eternal God to cry bitter tears! Can you imagine that, *bitter tears* on the face of the All-powerful God because of the unfaithfulness of His people? Divided hearts bring bitter tears.

Fast-forward to NT times and you find the Lord has chosen the same analogy to describe His relationship with His people.

Jesus Christ is the Bridegroom and every saved person on the planet is a part of the Bride. This is God's great way of describing the relationship He desires with us!

He wants an intimacy with us that only the closest of human relationships could picture correctly. He didn't say He wanted to be like close neighbors or even family. He didn't say He wanted to be like great friends. He repeatedly says (throughout different time periods of history) that His desire is to be like a Groom and a bride – the closest and most intimate of all human relationships.

I remember a friend whose girlfriend would come to visit from time to time. It was always a joy to see them walking together and talking together. Everyone knew that they intended to be married when the time was right. Time passed and we all went our separate ways. I learned later that they did marry, and also that my friend had discovered that his new bride had been in an adulterous relationship with another man for many years. I can only imagine the *bitter tears* that were cried by this young man who had a heart to serve the Lord. He watched his marriage disintegrate before his eyes.

Too often in life we haven't needed to imagine the pain of unfaithfulness. It's been right there in front of us as we have tried to be a comfort to those whose father, mother or spouse had forsaken them. I have held ones that I love as they cry and physically shake because of the unfaithfulness of family members. I have prayed for those who weep at night because of the horrific pain of the betrayal of their spouse. I have heard of ones I love who drove around for three days contemplating ending their life because of pain from betrayal.

Some time ago, I sat for a full afternoon across from a young husband, trying to convince him to forsake his selfish desires and to love his wife and five kids. Today they are divorced and live hundreds of miles apart.

The point is this; the marriage relationship is how the Living God has chosen to reveal His heart to us! He wants the most intimate of relationships with us and when the one He loves doesn't have a focused pure love in return, it affects Him similarly to the way it affects us! It puts *bitter tears* on the face of God.

In James 4:1-4, the Lord identifies four major issues among His people: covetousness, prayerlessness, selfishness, and worldliness. Please notice what the people who practice these things are called! He calls them "Adulterers and Adulteresses!" Wow! Because we know people affected by adultery, we typically find it easy to hate that sin of adultery. That sin has deeply affected so many families! It is easy to get angry at that sin, and we're not wrong to be angry.

"Hate evil you who love the Lord." Psalm 97:10

We get angry at the tears that adultery causes and the shattered lives that have to be started over. We get angry at the fact that parents can up and start over while their kids have to suffer their parent's carnal behavior for life. The Lord says, *"I hate the work of those who fall away."* (Psalm 101:3b) (Please note that it doesn't say I hate the workers who fall away, but their works, i.e., the sin itself.) We don't have a hard time hating the sin of adultery!

The thing that hits me like a falling piano is this. When I read through this passage honestly and humbly, I realize *I am the adulterer* this passage is describing! Covetousness has all too often characterized my walk in my years of knowing Jesus Christ as Savior. Prayerlessness has been a major theme of decades of my Christian life. I would be so much more disgustingly selfish than I still am if it were not for the goodness of God wooing me to better ways than what I would naturally choose for myself.

Friendship with the world was a conscious goal of mine as a fifteen-year-old football player in high school. At that point in my Christian life, I made a conscience choice not to say much about Jesus Christ. I knew very well that to speak that Name, and to seek to be a witness for Him, meant not being in the accepted social circle. So I made a choice. *"Don't say so much about Christ,"* I thought. *"Try to swear a couple times to fit in,"* I told myself. I didn't even know these verses existed at that time, yet I was actively and consciously seeking to do one of the things these verses condemn – being friends with the world.

In that same season of life there was a friend named Leann who went to the same church growing up and also to the same

15

high school. She really loved the Lord Jesus and was a great example to many of us. She came walking down the hall one day with a few friends as I was standing around with my freshman football player buddies. I heard her mention the name Jesus. I don't think I had any physical outward reaction, but I will never forget the cringing in my heart when she said that. I knew that to be identified with that Name meant not being cool. I was ashamed of a Savior who has never been ashamed of me, and now I'm ashamed that I was ashamed. Wow, how much I have been forgiven! Thank You, Lord, for grace and mercy!

It's one thing to be righteously angry at the sin of adultery, and it's another thing altogether to admit that I'm the adulterer this passage is describing! We're not only far too often victims of this horrific sin and its miserable and hurtful consequences, but also guilty ourselves of this horrific sin. Man, I don't like that, but it's true, if I take the word of God seriously. I don't like being called an adulterer. It's hard to hear that my covetousness, prayerlessness, selfishness, and worldliness in God's eyes are looked upon as cheating on His Son. God, help us, starting with me, to humble ourselves, to agree with Him, to see as He sees, to tremble before His word, and to repent everywhere it shines on our ugly sin.

---

*Selah (pause and think about it) – take time
to pray, to be in the Lord's presence as long
as He directs.*

Now we must take the final step. As we have noted, it's one thing to be angry at adultery, and it's another step to admit that at one time or another in our Christian lives this cheating characterized us. We must, if we are to heed what the

Lord is saying here, be willing to stand like Ezra and say, *"Here we are before you, in our guilt."* (Ezra 9:15b)

My dear Christian friend, my brother and sister, are you currently cheating on your relationship with Jesus Christ through covetousness, prayerlessness, selfishness, and/or worldliness? Are you willing to agree with God about your sin? Are you willing to see it the way He sees it? Are you willing to turn to God from your sin and call it what He calls it, to ask Him to cleanse you, and to purpose by grace to stop cheating on His Son? *"If we confess our sins, He is faithful and just to forgive us our sins, and to cleanse us from all unrighteousness."* (1 John 1:9) If you are willing to admit that you have been cheating, please, on behalf of Jesus Christ, I plead with you to deal with it right now. Get alone with the Lord. Get on your face before the Lord and make things right for the pleasure of our God, for the glory of our worthy God, and also for your eternal blessing.

Please know that there is no assumption that every Christian is cheating on the Lord Jesus through these or other besetting sins, nor that everyone who reads this book needs to repent. But at the same time, having had the privilege of traveling among the people of God in North America for over twenty years, it has become so clear these days that we, as the Bride of Christ, are in a state of spiritual adultery and are in great need of repentance that will leads us into revival.

It would not be OK with me if my wife cheated on me. It would not be OK with me if my future son-in-law or daughter-in-law cheated on one of my kids. It would not be OK with me if one of my friends' spouses decided to cheat on them. And, it is not OK for the Bride of Christ, through being covetous, prayerless, selfish, and worldly, to cheat on the lovely One of the heavens. We cannot be OK with the Bride of Christ in North America having a divided love that breaks the heart of our Savior. Things must change. We must be changed. We must repent. Lord, help us.

Steps Toward Purity
What do we do? How do we get there?

1. ***Wash Your Mind.*** Perhaps you are familiar with the phrase *"wash your mind with the water of the Word."* This is what the Lord desires to do for His Bride: *"that He might sanctify and cleanse her with the washing of water by the word."* Ephesians 5:26

There are good reasons that we quote and re-quote such verses. The first and most essential step leading us into a life of purity is to regularly spend time in God's Word! Christians in North American are not suffering, for the most part, because we do not understand this principle. Rather, we are spiritually distressed for not applying this principle to our lives! (*"Blessed are those who hear the word of God and keep it!"* (Luke 11:28)

My father, whom I deeply love, is perfect. Not everyone can say they have a perfect father, but I can. He became perfect a number of years ago when cancer took over his body and he was called Home to be with the Savior he loved. The only thing you had to do to make my dad cry in the last ten years of his life was say something nice about Jesus Christ. When you did, he would tear up and say, "Amen," with a joyful, broad smile. I remember him also crying with me privately one time and telling me that the biggest mistake of his entire life was not spending more time in God's Word. He was a humble man. He knew his sin and the sins of his kids and he knew it could have been different if he had been "nourished up" (1 Timothy 4:6) in the Word as the leader of the family. He purposed to change this in the last decade of his life, and by grace he did. I would call him and say, "Hi dad, what are you doing?" He would respond, "Ezekiel!" with a joyful laugh on the other end of the phone. He lived, as I have lived, with times of dryness and separation from God's Word, and he also lived with wonderful times of joyful intimacy with the Lord. If we are seeking to live a life of purity, the number one thing we can do is to spend time with the Living Word of God (Jesus Christ) through the written Word of God!

2. Take Heed. *"How can a young man cleanse his way? By taking heed according to Your Word."* Psalm 119:9

How can we take steps toward living pure lives with and for Him? Step 2 is to *take heed*. Don't just hear God's Word, or read God's Word, but read it with a heart to heed anything and everything you come to see through it! Application is the final and essential step of any profitable Bible reading or study!

Sadly, there are numerous men who have preached the Word of God, and know it very well, who are, or have just finished, sitting in prison as a result of their sinful lack of purity. Reading the Word is necessary. Reading to HEED IT will cleanse our way!

Do you remember David's mighty men being with him in the cave of Adullam? That is an amazing story. The rejected king, in a sort of off-handed comment says, "If I could only have a drink from the well of Bethlehem." The mighty men look at each other and, abruptly decided to venture into the enemy's stronghold to get David a drink from that well. What an example for the people of God! We must earnestly pray that the Bride of Christ will have that kind of heart!

We must read the Word of God with a heart that says, "Anything the rejected King says in this book that will delight His heart, I will spend the rest of my life doing for His pleasure and Glory."

We need to replace 'what suits me' with a life of reading and heeding what suits Christ! Read and heed, we must be those that read and heed.

3. ***Keep Oneself Unspotted.*** *"Pure and undefiled religion before God and the Father is this: to visit orphans and widows in their trouble, and to keep oneself unspotted from the world."* James 1:27

Step 3 is to make a conscious, purposeful choice to keep yourself from the things of the world that are spotting the people of God in North America. This in itself is a huge task given the corrupt society we live in, and please don't only think of the unsaved culture of the world! It is the Christian culture that must change. Sadly, it has become normal, publicly acceptable, and even applaudable to laugh at and pay money for things that caused Jesus Christ to suffer on the cross! We are finding great humor and pleasure in things that are deeply offensive to Jesus Christ. We are laughing at and participating in specific things that caused the suffering of One we say that we love and want to give ourselves for! My dearly loved brothers and sisters, how can these things be? How can we be okay with this?

We were at a North American Bible camp a number of years ago standing with several counselors and also a good number of the high school campers for the week, when two counselors began to discuss a popular movie that had recently been released. One of the counselors looked over to the other and loudly and unashamedly said, "Did you see that movie?" and the other responded, "Yes I did. Best movie I ever saw in my life!"

I was standing to the side watching this whole scene. It was Sunday afternoon, the day the campers were arriving to spend the week. The camp staff had been praying that the Lord would work powerfully in the campers' lives. Here were two young people seeking to spend their week in service to the Living God openly and unashamedly talking about a movie that was utterly defiling. I know this because when I heard about the movie it sounded like it might be interesting to me, too. I like that particular kind of movie so I visited a couple trustworthy websites that provide movie reviews to help people, like me, determine if we should watch something or not. Frankly, I felt defiled just reading information about the movie. I exited the webpage after reading a few lines; the movie clearly contained pornographic material!

How did we get to the place where we are okay laughing at and spending money on things that are so offensive to our Savior?

The answer to that question is really quite simple. We have been following culture in North America down a moral slope of degeneration for a long, long time. We have not been holding ourselves to the standards in God's Word but rather to the standards common to our North American culture composed of saved and unregenerate souls. God's Word says that we (every Christian, not just some extreme type of Christian) are to keep ourselves unspotted from the things of the world. We have simply *not been doing that*. We have been finding pleasure in things that are not funny. We have been paying for and hence supporting things that caused Jesus Christ suffering on His cross and that are still deeply offensive to Him now!

Please see, dear friend, that this is the state that we are in as the Bride of Christ on this continent. We have far too long been participating in things that mock and are deeply offensive to our Lord. We cannot continue in this carnal delusional

21

thinking! We must repent of this part of what has become normal to us! We must keep ourselves unspotted from the things of the world!

The Bible doesn't state a case against movies. It does against believers partaking in filth! It doesn't state a case against family movie nights. It does against drinking in the things that plant wicked ideas in our kids' (and our) heads. It doesn't speak against Hollywood. It does against enjoying things that mock Jesus Christ and against participating in and giving our money to things that serve to further an agenda that ultimately hurts people precious to Jesus Christ and robs Him of what He deserves! So, let's not be against theaters. Let's be against us being OK with things that He is not OK with, of not even giving filth a second thought because of a seared conscience! We must come to the place that we love what He loves and hate what He hates! We must examine our conduct and ask the Lord what is offensive to Him and *repent* (turn to God from our sin). If it mocks Him, we cannot be OK with it or be willing to enjoy it. If it added to His suffering, how can we want it to add to our pleasure? If it is offensive to Him now, why is it not offensive to us? We must love Him more than we love the passing pleasures of sin or the entanglements of this world! **This is the way FORWARD!**

I thank the Lord for and pray for the groups of Christians that have been led of the Lord to make movies! Please be rabidly true to Jesus Christ, my movie making friends! Please stand unwaveringly for what is right, both when it's popular and if and when it's not! I pray for you, my movie making brothers and sisters! Press on *and never* compromise! I thank God for you!

Movies are only one area of many that a serious Christ follower must allow the Lord to bring into submission to His perfect will. Movies are being discussed because they are such a prevalent example in our culture, but it would be sad if readers thought only of this one area of life. Please don't limit your holy consecration to movie watching only. We must prayerfully think through everything in our lives and ask the all-knowing Spirit of God to search us and show us the ways that we are not, *"keeping ourselves unspotted from the things of the world."* God's Word says that this is true religion. So, dearly loved Christian, how true is your religion? Are you willing to repent of what the Lord shows you and to ask and seek by His grace to be changed? Are you willing to be brought into greater blessing than you have chosen for yourself so far? Earnestly praying that it will be so.

4. Meditate On Pure Things. *"Whatever things are pure... meditate on these things."* Philippians 4:8

Having removed the things that are spotting the lives of the Bride of Christ in point #3, we now find that the vacuum needs to be filled lest other equally unworthy or worse come in to rob, steal, and kill the spiritual vitality of the Bride on this continent. 1 John 3:3 says, *"Everyone who has this hope in Him purifies himself, just as He is pure."* In other words, if you are thinking on Jesus Christ and His return, if you are seeking those things that are above, then there will be a purifying effect in your life.

This focusing on right and holy things begins with the reading of God's Word every morning. How many of the Bride of Christ in our land would be in need of the same rebuke the Lord gave His people in Jeremiah 7:13?

"I spoke to you, rising up early and speaking, but you did not hear, and I called you, but you did not answer."

23

I spent my high school years involved in different services for the Lord most nights of the week, yet I spent very little time sitting at His feet through His Word and allowing Him to love me and commune with me. My battle with thinking on pure things and honoring Him with my mind would have been so greatly helped had I been feeding on His Word and putting pure and holy things into my mind every morning.

Please do this not only for yourselves, but also see to it that the ones the Lord has put in your care are starting their days nourished with the good Word of God. Some day you will give an account of all the Lord has entrusted to you. This is a simple and absolutely essential part of doing well and leading well.

5. **Be The Friend Of The One Who Loves Purity.** *"He who loves purity of heart and has grace on his lips, the king will be his friend."* Proverbs 22:11

What an amazing verse! Notice how it says this *person loves* purity of heart! We so need people like that! And please, also notice that it says that the king will be the friend of the one who loves purity of heart. The Lord eagerly encourages us to have the same heart in us that this king has! Whoever we find that loves purity, let's be their friend. Let's love them and encourage them and side with them. People who love purity, especially young people, but really all people, need friends! It can be, and many times is, a lonely road when a Christian chooses to love purity and turn away from the things that dishonor the Lord Jesus. Many people, and sometimes most, are not willing to choose such a biblical standard (may the Lord change this through revival).

I have a dear friend, Dan, who had great biblically based standards in high school about many things. One time a large group of us from our youth group were together and the group decided to head off to an activity that is perhaps permissible, but is definitely questionable. Without giving it a second thought I was going to go with them, when I noticed that my friend Dan was saying goodbye to people. I asked him privately what he was doing, and he quietly stated that he had decided before the Lord not to participate in such things, so he was headed home.

Well, all of a sudden, I had a choice. Would I see the one who loved purity, who was willing to stand on his own in honor of the Word, and side with him, or would I go with the crowd?

I knew in an instant what I should do – be a friend to the one who held the high biblical standard! (Thank you Lord for grace and the ministry of the Holy Spirit!) So, before I even knew the Scriptures myself, and before I had real standards of my own, and for sure before I knew this verse, I became the friend of the one who loved purity. How thankful I am for that! And, this friend became my best childhood friend. I eventually named my son after him and now serve the Lord full time with him! He is still my best buddy today, a lifelong gift from the Lord! What blessing flows from obeying the Scripture, God help us!

This is a small example of what Scripture is encouraging all Christ-loving disciples to do. Band together and love those who love purity. We are to value Christians more than our Christian liberty (Romans 14; 1 Corinthians 6-9). Choose the sometimes radical counter-cultural practice of a life of holy living! Look for those who take purity for Christ seriously, and please be the friend of the one who is striving for biblical purity (not the legalistic counterfeit)!

6. Be An Example. *"Be an example to the believers in…
purity."* 1 Timothy 4:12

In this verse the Lord once again raises the bar. Not only
should we be having our minds washed, taking heed to the
standards of God's Word, not only should we keep ourselves
unspotted and think on pure things, not only should we be a
friend to the one who loves purity, but we are to be an
example of purity. If we take the time to think this through,
that is quite a standard! This means we need to be setting our
standard based on the youngest and weakest of the Christians,
not on what we think does or does not affect us. If everyone in
our local church were following us, what would be the most
Christ-honoring standard we could choose? From the least
mature of those who will read this book to the most mature,
we must all take our place and say that we have a long way to
go to be conformed to the image of the spotless Lamb of God.
What must *change* or *go* in order for us to be the example of
purity the Lord would have us to be?

If we are respectable at all, and are participating in church
life the way the Scripture describes, then eventually people will
come to us and say things such as, "What do you do when such
and such a situation comes up?" Your answer to that question
affects the holiness and purity of the local church. We need to
tremble when we interact with Christians, those so precious to
Jesus Christ. My saved friend, deeply loved of God, I beg you,
beseech you, plead with you, and implore you, please be an
example to the believers in purity! This next generation needs
men and women who won't compromise, men and women
who love the Lord Jesus more than they love anything else and
who order their lives in holiness and purity!

We talked earlier in the chapter about James 4, the
adulterers and adulteresses of that day who were told to
submit, resist, draw near, cleanse, purify, lament, mourn and

weep. (see James 4:4-10) If you recognize a lack of purity in your life that grieves the heart of your Savior, please get on your face before God and do not just look in the mirror and walk away unchanged. The wise man hears God's Word and does what it says. The fool also hears God's Word but walks away unwilling to be brought into a place of greater blessing and conformity to what the Word says. I pray that the adulterers and adulteresses of our day (starting with me!) will repent with tears and that times of refreshing will come from the Lord all through North America. God, help us!

Do you remember the woman in Mark 14:3-9 who poured out her alabaster flask of costly oil? I understand the oil she anointed the Lord with was worth approximately one year's salary. Years ago, the average annual salary from where I come from in the Midwest was around $40,000 a year. I have read that story in Mark 14 many times and wondered if the Lord would ever give me the privilege of making an offering like that, $40,000 that I could pour out unto Him however He directed me. Well, these days I read that story and I have been brought to realize that I have already been given something the Lord says is infinitely more valuable than $40,000. I have me. I have my life. The Lord Jesus calls me His bride and reminds me in hundreds of ways both through His Word and through the details of my life that He cherishes me. I have the privilege, through His grace, of being a pure offering that would honor Him and that is a greater privilege than just giving Him money. Listen to what the Lord says in Romans 12:1-2:

---

*"I beseech you therefore, brethren, by the
mercies of God that you present your bodies
a living sacrifice, holy, acceptable to God,
which is your reasonable service. And do not*

> be conformed to this world, but be
> transformed by the renewing of your mind,
> that you may prove what is that good and
> acceptable and perfect will of God."

Please, my dear brothers and sisters in Christ, we must be a pure offering poured out to the Lord. How many marriages have to fail before we realize that we are being deeply hurt by the standards we have chosen? How much longer must the HOLY SPIRIT of God who indwells every believer be forced to live with a lack of purity which grieves His heart? Please, repent. Please, confess. Please, be changed and allow the Lord to bring you into the blessing He longs for, the blessing of being an *example to the Believers in purity*.

The Promise of Purity

What honors and pleases Jesus Christ must be the foremost motivation we have as the North American Bride of Christ. But, although that should always be enough, the Bible adds other motivations to consider as well. There are promises of blessing to those who choose a life of purity. As we close this chapter, consider a few of God's promises.

> "Who may ascend into the hill of the Lord? Or who may stand in His holy place? He who has clean hands and a pure heart, who has not lifted up his soul to an idol, nor sworn deceitfully. He shall receive blessing from the Lord...." Psalm 24:3-5a

Notice the words "ascend" and "stand." These words speak to us of being where He is, dwelling with Him. We might say this is a promise of intimacy with Him. The one who has clean hands and a pure heart can dwell with a God of infinite holiness. This one shall receive blessing from the Lord.

It's appropriate to note here that none of us, that is *none of us*, would ever have any semblance of purity if it were not for the grace of God. A Holy God views our best acts of righteousness, apart from the blood of Jesus Christ, as filthy rags (Isaiah 64:6). We are utterly dependent on Him and Him alone for purity, both positionally at salvation, and practically as we carry on in our Christian life. But the Scripture quickly adds to this thought, that once we are saved, bathed, justified, judicially declared righteous, or however else you want to say it, we can and do make many decisions that affect our practical and filial relationship with the Lord. In other words, you can be declared righteous and also have your life contain things that are grievous to the Lord.

"Blessed are the pure in heart, for they shall see God."
Matthew 5:8

Again, a promise of intimacy for the one who chooses a life of purity! So how does that sound? Our eternal occupation will be Jesus Christ! Our eternal life doesn't start the day we die; it starts the day we are born again! The blessed man is the one who is taken up with Jesus Christ now and lives for Him in all things! Paul says it this way, *"Therefore we make it our aim, whether present or absent, to be well pleasing to Him."* (2 Corinthians 5:9) Do you believe the Lord is right when He says that a life of Christ-like purity is the most blessed life one can have?

> *The enemy has always been telling the same lies that he is telling today. "The Lord doesn't want the best for you," (has God said you can't eat of every tree of the garden?), he says to the followers of God. "There won't be consequences," he whispers in the ears of unsuspecting sheep. "If you sin, life will be better and this sin will open you up to greater things than what you are capable of enjoying now," he so despicably suggests.*

Please, don't listen to the lies of one who comes to destroy lives. Honor the Living Word of God, Jesus Christ, by honoring the written Word of God. Rather than explaining it away or living in compromise, allow your life to be radically changed for His pleasure and glory and your eternal blessing!

So, we can clearly see that God is pure, and that we must be pure. There are biblical steps to take toward purity, and amazing blessings for those who take the Lord at His Word and submit their lives to His best! Lord, help us!

I would sooner be holy than happy if the two things could be divorced. Were it possible for a man always to sorrow and yet to be pure, I would choose the sorrow if I might win the purity, for to be free from the power of sin, to be made to love holiness, is true happiness.

— Charles Spurgeon

We Must Be Prayerful

Prayer has divided seas, rolled up flowing flooded rivers, made flinty rocks gush into fountains, quenched flames of fire, muzzled lions, disarmed vipers and poisons, marshaled the stars against the wicked, stopped the source of the moon, arrested the sun in its great race, burst open iron gates, recalled souls from eternity, conquered the strongest devils, commanded legions of angels down from heaven. Prayer has bridled and changed the raging passions of men, and routed and destroyed vast armies of proud daring blustering atheists. Prayer has brought one man from the bottom of the sea, and carried another in a chariot to heaven, what has not prayer done!

— William MacDonald

I would rather pray than seek to solve all the mysteries of prayer.
— Unknown

What is Prayer?

Prayer is Christ. Prayer is a love relationship with Christ. Prayer is the overflow of a love relationship with Christ. It's hard to express how much I've missed the boat when it comes to this subject of prayer and how much I regret that. Also, hard to put into words is how much I long to press on into all that the Lord has for me in this realm, and how much I hunger for and pray for God's people to enter in as well.

Prayer is communion with God, and as such is the greatest joy of life now and will be the greatest joy of our unending eternity with Him in the life to come. There is no greater joy or privilege in this life, or in the next, than to fellowship with God.

That is what prayer is: fellowship with the most amazing Person that any of us will ever know!

It is mind blowing what the Scriptures describe in the vast subject of prayer; the privilege of it, the power of it, the personal relationship of it. I know so many preachers who are great with their Bibles and strong in their studies, yet each man would tell you that they have really fallen short when it came to the *living out of prayer* and that their lives and their ministries consequently paid the price, and their reward at the judgment seat of Christ will reflect that loss. (This is so sobering. God, help us)

The admonitions to be a Christlike people of prayer are everywhere in Scripture. It is sad that so many of us know the verses, have expounded the verses, yet have not lived out their simple instructions. The subject of prayer is difficult. We struggle with guilt and misconceptions concerning prayer. Most Christians would tell you they think they ought to pray more and feel guilty that they don't. Somehow (by God's grace!) we must grasp the fact that prayer is not a *task* to be completed, but a love relationship to be enjoyed! It is not a discipline to be guilty over, but an invitation to be passionately pursued! God, help us to see prayer the way that Christ did, to make it the same priority that He did, and to come into the benefits of it the same way as well!!

Are We Serious About Prayer?

Ok, let's jump in asking the Lord to please work in our lives.

"Therefore be serious and watchful in your prayers." 1 Peter 4:7b

Let's ask ourselves a question in response to God's Word: Are we serious about prayer? (This is about the simplest response to God's Word that we could have. The verse says "be serious." So, are we serious?) Would someone who knows all the habits of your life and every detail of the way you choose to spend your time, come to the conclusion that you are serious (disciplined and self-restrained) when it comes to your prayer life? If serious is not the way you would honestly be described, are you willing for the Lord to work in your life and make you serious about prayer?

If not, then right from the start, are you willing to be honest with God about that failing? Are you willing to let God change you? If you're not, then how can God help you? There is a world full of people that He longs to bless, and prayer would be one of the greatest ways of blessing them, but He's not a bully. He invites people to God-sized blessing. *"Everyone who thirsts, come to the waters; and you who have no money, come, buy and eat. Yes, come buy wine and milk without money and without price. Why do you spend money for what is not bread, and your wages for what does not satisfy? Listen carefully to Me, and eat what is good, and let your soul delight itself in abundance."* (Isaiah 55:1-2) He stands at the door and knocks (Revelation 3:20), but if we persist in our own will, He politely gives preference to us and turns us over to our own counsel. *"But My people would not heed My voice, and Israel would have none of Me. So I gave them over to their own stubborn heart, to walk in their own counsels."* (Psalm 81:1-2)

---

*How it breaks the heart of God to want better
things for us than we will accept (see Luke 19:41).*

Lord, help us to be willing, and at the very least to pray, Lord, I'm willing to be made willing. Please make me willing!

For those who have the responsibility of leadership in the local church, please apply the same question corporately that has just been asked and applied individually. Is your local church serious (disciplined and self-restrained) about prayer? The prayer meeting in the churches of North American took a turn toward non-existence a long time ago. It is normal for many, many churches across this land to have little or no time set aside for corporate prayer anymore. If you are part of a local church that has little or no prayer, are you willing to agree with Scripture and admit at the beginning of this chapter, that the Lord needs to revive this part of your group? I hope so! When we see that we are falling short of the standards of God's Word and are willing to repent, confess, and be changed, that leads us down a path of incredible blessing!

I spoke with a friend from Ontario this morning who told me how months ago his father had attended a conference where I had the privilege of speaking. There he heard the message that is the basis of this chapter. Through the Lord's working in his life, he left the conference that day under great conviction that their local church had been fruitless in the kids' work they had been doing, and what needed to happen was for him and another brother in the church to meet and pray the whole time the kids' work was going on. They began to do this, meeting weekly to pray in another room while the kids' work was going on. Fast-forward a couple of months to this morning when I was speaking again with my friend. He reported that in the last few weeks they have seen fifteen clear professions of faith in the Lord Jesus accompanied by the fruit of changed lives! *"Ask and it will be given to you."* (Matthew 7:7) Praise the Lord for the power of prayer! The ministry went from fruitlessness to fruitfulness because of repentance and simple obedience to God's Word! Praise the Lord that we have a God who is eager to bring us into more blessing if we will only be honest and humble before His Word and allow Him to have His way in our lives!

My dear brother or sister in Christ, do you want to be blessed? Do you want to live a zealous, fruitful life that you can give an account of with joy at the Judgment seat of Christ? If so, you must be a person of devoted, disciplined, and serious prayer!

If we are going to reach North America with the gospel of Jesus Christ in this next generation, we must be a people of prayer! As was shared in the introduction, if your body stops talking to your head, you are in *huge* trouble! Spiritually it is no different! If we stop talking to our Head, we are in *huge* trouble! We must, must, must be a people of prayer!

To get the greatest profit out of this chapter, please pause to pray, asking the Lord to open His Word to you, and then read and meditate on Ephesians 3:14-21

For this reason I bow my knees to the Father of our Lord Jesus Christ, from whom the whole family in heaven and earth is named, that He would grant you, according to the riches of His glory, to be strengthened with might through His Spirit in the inner man, that Christ may dwell in your hearts through faith; that you, being rooted and grounded in love, may be able to comprehend with all the saints

35

what is the width and length and depth and height — to know the love of Christ which passes knowledge; that you may be filled with all the fullness of God. Now to Him who is able to do exceedingly abundantly above all that we ask or think, according to the power that works in us, to Him be glory in the church by Christ Jesus to all generations, forever and ever. Amen.

Growing In Power, Intimacy, and Knowledge

1. **A Biblical Stance of Prayer.** *"For this reason I bow my knees to the Father of our Lord Jesus Christ."* Ephesians 3:14

Please note that I didn't say the biblical stance of prayer. There are many biblical stances of prayer (prostrate, sitting, standing, raising holy hands, etc...). This is just one of them, and it happens to be my favorite right now.

Notice the phrase, *"bow my knees."* We tend to get on our knees only in serious situations. We don't get down on our knees all the time. Being on our knees would indicate dependence, humility, consecration, earnestness, and fervency, just to start. We are currently, suffering deeply because of a great lack of prayer, but we are incapable of recognizing it. One of the characteristics of the lukewarm church is blindness (see Revelation 3:14-22). The solution to spiritual blindness is prayer! (*"The eyes of your understanding being enlightened."* (Ephesians 1:18) It's ironic that the solution to prayerlessness is prayer! The Apostle Paul sets a wonderful example when he says to the Ephesian Christians that he will be "bowing his knees" before God in prayer. We would be smart to think the same and to copy his example!

I had the privilege of being with a church elder, on our knees, when he began to cry before the Lord and say to the

Lord, "I don't know how you could use someone like me, but please use me to reach someone with the gospel of Jesus Christ." This elder is a humble man who meant every word he was saying. He felt a great sense of his own dependence on the Lord in order to be used in evangelism.

Well, a number of weeks later a young man approached him at work and began to ask him questions about the Lord. The elder had a great conversation that day, and pointed this young man to an evangelistic Bible study that had started a few weeks earlier. About two months into the study this young man came to Christ and then he led his wife to Christ! What a joy and a blessing for me to see the whole process: from a humble man of God on his knees asking for what we know is the Lord's will, to seeing disciples made and brought into the group! Praise the Lord!

2. **Power Leading to Intimacy.** *"…to be strengthened with might (power) through His Spirit…"* Ephesians 3:16b

Where are we to get the *power* to live the Christian life? How are we to love the Lord with *all*? How are we to love our spouses so selflessly, and our neighbors so humbly? The answer is simple and yet so vitally important. *We need power* from on high, and apart from Divine help and power we will live frustrated lives of failure and discouragement! Thank God that we have access to this help through prayer! Lord, help us to avail ourselves of it by coming, *"Boldly to the throne of grace that we may obtain mercy and find grace to help in time of need!"* (Hebrews 4:16)

"We never come closer to omnipotence than when we pray in Jesus Name."

What a privilege for little feeble people to be allowed through prayer to tap into Divine power. Wow!

Later in the book we will devote an entire chapter to the subject of power. The purpose in this chapter is to show the connection between prayer and power. God's power is unleashed, by His Sovereign choice, through prayer. He has spoken simply and straightforwardly. He sits on His throne of grace ready to dispense grace to help any who will come for it!

In the context of Paul's prayer, he requests power to produce intimacy. Note what Paul says, *"that Christ may dwell in your hearts through faith."* (Ephesians 3:17a) Is Paul praying that the Ephesian Christians would have Jesus come live in their hearts and thereby be saved? No! Of course not! He is praying for intimacy between the Lord Jesus and His people! He is not praying that the Lord Jesus would be present, but that He would be comfortable in every realm of the Believers' lives.

My wife and I are in our third decade of marriage. It has been a delight (with intermittent skirmishes) through every stage, and it just gets better as we go! I feel badly for people who jump into marriages, enjoying the social, emotional, and physical joys of marriage, but when they hit hard times they bail. They never experience the deepening joy and comfort of a stable and mature relationship! They miss out on so much of what the Lord created a lifelong partnership to be!

This is not meant as criticism. The breakdown of relationships is a heartbreaking problem, and there is such a parallel between that and what Paul is praying for here in this passage. He prays for the love relationship between the Lord Jesus and His people to grow and deepen. What a beautiful prayer!

I want a growing, thrilling, passionate, joyful, satisfying relationship with my wife! I want a growing, thrilling, passionate, joyful, satisfying relationship with my God! Any honest, Spirit-filled, Bible reader who carefully goes through the Scriptures sees that we have a God who wants to have a growing, thrilling, passionate, joyful, satisfying relationship with us! Wow! Praise the Lord!

Much of this quiet intimate place with our God expresses itself in prayer! Prayer is the overflow of a love relationship with Him. Lord, lead us on to know Him, dwell with Him in prayer, and allow Him the fellowship He desires with us!

Paul prays for power to be unleashed in the lives of Christians, showing itself specifically in a newfound intimacy between the Christian and Christ. Lord please help us to copy Paul's prayer for the Ephesian believers and to come into the good of it ourselves!!

3. **Intimacy Leads to Knowledge.** *"That you...may be able to comprehend with all the saints what is the width and length and depth and height."* Ephesians 3:18

Can you picture someone trying to understand things the way the Lord does? Well on the one hand, who sees like our God? Who thinks like Him? Who would ever be able to? God's Word reinforces this truth very clearly:

"For My thoughts are not your thoughts, nor are your ways My ways," says the Lord. *"For as the heavens are higher than the earth, so are My ways higher than your ways, and My thoughts than your thoughts."* Isaiah 55:8-9

Yet, in this passage you have a clear prayer of Paul's for greater understanding, greater comprehension, and, you could say, greater vision.

We often hear this verse quoted: *"Without vision the people perish."* (Proverbs 29:18) That's a great verse and such a needed truth. The problem is, we often confuse vision with creativity. We have to be very careful here. Vision is seeing how God sees! The Lord is a creative God, and I love and admire creative people, but when we speak of having "vision" in spiritual things, the idea is that we dwell in the intimate, quiet place with the Head of the Church, Jesus Christ the Lord; that we are sensitive to the guidance of the Holy Spirit of God who resides in every Believer; that we are in tune with Him to the degree that we think to an extent how He thinks, see how He sees, feel how He feels, and hence our perspective is in line with His! This is vision! Lord, help us to have true biblical vision and to see how He sees. Let's follow Christ's example and pray for this!

For years I had a deep burden for a community about an hour from where I used to live. At one point the Lord opened a door for me to spend two weeks there reaching out with the gospel with a team of young men. Since it is only an hour away, I decided it would be best to drive back and forth every day. Day one I jumped in my car, set out on my way, and before long I was weeping over the 13,000 souls who live there. I did the same on the way home. Now, if you know me, you would know that this is a work of God in my life. I have spent the great bulk of my life not weeping over lost souls, and my spiritual gift is really focused on the body of Christ. Well, I did the same thing day after day for those two weeks. Still to this day, it's hard to talk about that community without crying. I see them as sheep without a Shepherd, one breath and one heartbeat away from spending eternity in the Lake of Fire, separated from a loving God who has already paid the price for them. I see them chained to drugs, to sexual sin, to religious hypocrisy and pride. I know how badly they need the Lord Jesus, and it breaks my heart! (*"You must be born again!"* John 3:7)

In some small way the Lord is helping me see how He sees, think how He thinks, feel how He feels, etc. Lord, help me on.

Lord, help all of us on through prayer to share in His heart and mind!

4. **A Deeper Enjoyment of Him.** *"To know* (to experience through knowledge gained by experience) *the love of Christ which passes knowledge, that you may be filled with all the fullness of God."* Ephesians 3:19

We have a Savior who desires a relationship with us that He illustrates with the picture of marriage. (See the *whole* Bible) Paul here prays that the Christians will experience the love of Christ, and hence grow or "know" the love of Christ, which passes knowledge! What a privilege! What a joy! This blows away anything this world has to offer! We're brought into this incredible relationship with the King of kings and Lord of lords! His desire is for us! He wants us more than He wants our service! As hard as I try, I always seem to get that backwards, and I have the hardest time wrapping my feeble brain around the joy and wonder of this! This is what will truly satisfy our hearts! This is what we truly hunger for (even if we don't realize it)! *"That I may know Him."* Oh Lord, revive Your Church that we would lose our love for the world and love You as we ought!

The Lord has been so good and so kind. God's people could tell thousands upon thousands of stories of how delightful and kind and gracious and worthwhile He is to spend time with and to follow. Oh that the Lord would move in His power, so we would see the beauty of the Savior in a fresh way, and be caused to love Him with all. Lord, have Your way in us we pray!

As previously mentioned, my earthly father went home to be with the Lord a number of years ago. It was all such a whirlwind at the time. He had a cough that wouldn't go away. We didn't think anything of it at the time. Eventually, he would sometimes need to use oxygen, which of course was troubling, but we were all very hopeful that he would get better and didn't really think of any other possibility. I was with my family in North Carolina preaching and my mom let us know the doctor wanted to run several tests on my dad at the hospital on the Monday coming. Still, this wasn't overly troubling. The doctors explained that the medical tests could be accomplished more quickly at the hospital.

My father walked into the hospital and checked himself in on Monday morning as we were finishing our drive home from the weekend conference. We arrived home in the afternoon, literally threw our bags in the door and drove to the hospital. I rode the elevator up to his floor, walked a few steps into the hallway, saw my family in the waiting room, went straight to my mom and she collapsed into my arms weeping and thanking me for being there. Dad was having tests run at that point and I can't remember many more details from that day other than the whirlwind that started. Tuesday, my father, who worked hard all of his life, couldn't walk the eight steps to the bathroom any longer. Wednesday, they scheduled a lung biopsy. Thursday was the first time anybody said "cancer." Friday, they said, "We can't help him."

We walked back and told my dad what they had told us, and that unless the great and awesome God of the Heavens healed him, he was going to go and be with his God soon. He went to be with the Savior the next day, Saturday. Crazy week. Crazy experience. I told my wife all week I wanted to call a time out and sit and talk with my dad. Sometimes I wanted so badly to fight and save my dad from what was killing him. Sometimes I was numb. All through the week the Lord was so kind and so gracious and so present. I'm really trying to just tell you about one particular event I will never forget.

My dad went to his eternal home on Saturday night. I preached his funeral the following Wednesday morning. I slept only bits and pieces between those days. One night I was unable to sleep. I found myself sitting on my sofa at 3:30 a.m. trying to read my Bible, but I was not able to due to grief and tears. All my family was fast asleep. My heart was aching so badly, and I looked up to the ceiling and said,

---

"Lord, I need a hug. How do You hug people from heaven?"

"I know You love me, and I know You would be so willing, but how do you hug people when You are there and I'm here crying on my sofa?"

Then my phone buzzed. A note came in and the gist of it was this, "Hi Scott, my husband and I couldn't sleep, and we were laying here praying for you and we just wanted you to know that we love you and the Lord loves you."

Then my phone buzzed again. Another note came in, and while it was not word for word, the gist of it was the same. "We couldn't sleep. We were praying for you. We wanted to tell you we love you and the Lord loves you."

Then my phone buzzed once more. Another note came in and was very similar but added this, "Hi Scott, you probably won't get this until the morning, but we couldn't sleep. We were laying here praying for you and we wanted to go ahead and write you and tell you we love you and the Lord loves you."

I stopped counting after about 300 to 400 notes had been received over the next few days, and all of it began the instant that I asked the Lord in humble sincerity for a much needed hug. The hugs that came were so many that I gave my phone to my wife so I could deal with all the arrangements that needed to be cared for and to prepare to preach my dad's funeral.

So, what I'm trying to say is, for a long time I have believed the Lord loves me. I have experienced the love of God in many ways, but for me, weeping at 3:30 a.m. on my sofa with my heart exploding with sorrow, to be able to look up to the Lord, ask for a hug, and then see Him answer so resoundingly, clearly and instantly, was an experience of God's love that I will never forget!

This is just a small example of what Paul is praying for here for the people of God, that they would experientially know the love of Christ! I am so thankful for this sort of thing. The Lord Jesus is so close and so precious, and He desires such an intimate relationship with His people! I used to get lonely the instant friends would leave, and now I find myself so happy left "alone" with the friendship and companionship of my Savior. I cherish my time alone with Him and it's so hard to wrap my little head around the fact that He has been wooing me into this joyful, intimate relationship ever since I came to know Him all those years ago. Truly, in His presence is fullness of joy! What a privilege that we don't have to wait for eternity to enjoy our relationship with Him!

So, I pray today that you will experientially know the love of Christ in a greater way than ever before. Please trust Him! Pray this in faith, trusting that He knows how to love you and when to love you. Please don't read this and try to put Him in a box and tell Him how to show you His love. Just open yourself to Him, ask Him in simple trust and response to His Word, and watch Him love you with His wonderful creativity! I'm going to leave out most of the details, but I want to tell you I asked the Lord for a hug again several years after this story during a great trial.

I found myself at Psalm 145 in my Bible. Then the Lord showed me verse 18, *"The Lord is near to all who call upon Him, to all who call upon Him in truth."* It was like the Lord was telling me to take Him at His word. He couldn't be closer to me than what He was. I should trust that, believe that, strengthen myself in that, and press on. The first time I said I needed a hug, the Lord gave me one through His people. When I said it again, He knew I needed to be strengthened in His Word and believe Him at His word, so He gave that. His answers are perfect every time in both substance and timing. We must ask in faith, ask in dependence, ask knowing that what He sends and how He sends it will be perfect. Don't look for the Lord to do the same thing in your life that He has done in others' lives. Look for what He's uniquely eager to do in yours!

So, please see what the Lord has recorded here in the prayer of Paul. Pray along with what is recorded, trusting that the Lord is eager to fulfill His Word in His children's lives, and press on in the joyful intimacy that is still ahead as you walk your journey with Him! What a privilege!

Notice the result, *"That you may be filled with all the fullness of God."* (Ephesians 3:19b)

> The climax in this magnificent prayer is reached when Paul prays that you may be filled with (literal "unto," Gk. eis) all the fullness of God. All the fullness of the Godhead dwells in the Lord Jesus (Colossians 2:9). The more He dwells in our hearts by faith, the more we are filled unto all the fullness of God. We could never be filled with all the fullness of God. But it is a goal toward which we move.[1]

What a prayer! That He would grant you to be strengthened (with power). That Christ may dwell in your hearts (intimacy). And then the finale, that you may be filled with all the fullness of God. I love the way Paul prays! We have missed out on so much due to pitiful prayer lives! Lord, help us on!

5. Closing Praises. *"Now to Him who is able to do exceedingly abundantly above all that we ask or think, according to the power that works in us, to Him be glory in the Church by Christ Jesus to all generations, forever and ever. Amen."* Ephesians 3:20-21

At this point in Paul's prayer, he has asked for some huge things, and he directs our attention to the God who can easily answer these massive requests! I found this helpful in following Paul's doxology:

Able
Able to do
Able to do what we ask
Able to do what we think
Able to do what we ask or think
Able to do all that we ask or think
Able to do above all that we ask or think
Able to do abundantly above all that we ask or think
Able to do exceedingly abundantly above all that we ask or think[2]

He points us to the God who is able – I pray we never forget that. Our God is able! (powerful, skillful) What trust we should have in Him! What confidence we should live our lives with! How eager we should be to seek Him in prayer!

So far, this chapter has been focused on just one of Paul's prayers, and we have far from exhausted it, but there is a Bible full of beautiful prayers to learn from. This one prayer is simply used to illustrate the beauty and joy and privilege and *necessity* of praying Biblically! If we are going to see a work of God in our day on our island (North America) we must be a people of prayer! The Lord repeatedly commands us to be such a people in His Word.

- The **activity** of prayer; continue earnestly in prayer (Colossians 4:2)
- The **relationship** of prayer; pray without ceasing (I Thessalonians 5:17)
- The **attitude** of prayer; be serious in your prayer (I Peter 4:7)
- The **partnership** of prayer; I beg you to strive with me in prayer (Romans 15:30)

Prayer has been such an amazingly joyful journey that it's hard to stop the chapter at this point.

I've never discovered anything more delightful, fulfilling, thrilling, or difficult than letting the Lord grow my prayer life as I obey the biblical admonitions to pray and grow towards the goal of a Christlike life of prayer!

I'm such a child on this journey but growing is such a delight! Lord, help us on to all He has for us in this life of prayer!

Nowhere can we get to know the holiness of God, and come under His influence and power, except in the inner chamber. It has been well said: "No man can expect to make progress in holiness who is not often and long alone with God."
— Andrew Murray

We Must Be Passionate

Jesus Christ was, is, and ever will be passionate. He is passionate about the glory of God, the people of God, the work of God, the agenda of God, etc. There are a million plus things about Christ that are worship-worthy, and this is certainly one of them! Sold out, passionate, unyielding, all-in, how can we not admire Someone like that? What a privilege to have a leader like that!

The Lord's Example of Zeal

Do you remember when the Lord overthrew the money tables in the temple in John 2? Speaking of Him, the Word says, *"Zeal for Your house will consume me."* John 2:17 The Lord Jesus was and is a man's man. There was nothing wimpy about Him. From His fearless standing up to religious and secular leaders, to His fashioning a whip and overthrowing the tables of those who were using the House of God to make a profit, His life and His teaching from birth to death shows He was sold out, He was fearless, He was radically different than the men of His day. He was a zealous, admirable example for us to follow.

Think of the way He spoke. *"Pick up your cross and follow Me."* (Luke 9:23) *"No one can be My disciple unless he forsakes all and follows Me."* (Luke 14:33) He encouraged people to leave everything and follow Him. The Lord told them it would be so worth it when they did!

Zeal typified His life and ministry. I love this about our Savior, a leader who is worthy of absolute devotion.

The Lord Demands Our Zeal

In the book of Revelation, this same Savior is seen walking through the churches of that day, and for each one He has a message that is so wonderfully recorded for our benefit. To the church at Laodicea, the last one on the list, He deals with their lack of zeal:

> [14] *"And to the [angel of the church of the Laodiceans write, 'These things says the Amen, the Faithful and True Witness, the Beginning of the creation of God:* [15] *"I know your works, that you are neither cold nor hot. I could wish you were cold or hot.* [16] *So then, because you are lukewarm, and neither cold nor hot, I will vomit you out of My mouth.* [17] *Because you say, 'I am rich, have become wealthy, and have need of nothing'—and do not know that you are wretched, miserable, poor, blind, and naked —* [18] *I counsel you to buy from Me gold refined in the fire, that you may be rich; and white garments, that you may be clothed, that the shame of your nakedness may not be revealed; and anoint your eyes with eye salve, that you may see.* [19] *As many as I love, I rebuke and chasten. Therefore be zealous and repent.* [20] *Behold, I stand at the door and knock. If anyone hears My voice and opens the door, I will come in to him and dine with him, and he with Me.* [21] *To him who overcomes I will grant to sit with Me on My throne, as I also overcame and sat down with My Father on His throne.* [22] *"He who has an ear, let him hear what the Spirit says to the churches." Revelation 3:14-22*

What did the Lord Jesus want the church at Laodicea to understand? First, He reveals Himself to them (v. 14). Second,

He identifies their problem (v. 15). Third, He says how He feels about their spiritually lethargic and materialistic state (v. 16). Fourth, He counsels them as to what to do (v. 18). Fifth, He reassures them of His love and then He shows them what would happen if they obey Him (vv. 19-21). Man, we are richer for having this little portion of God's Word available to us. Please pause and pray (like right now!) then read this little passage (like right now!) then let's jump in asking the Lord to have His way with us the same way He was seeking to have His way with the Church of so long ago!

Who is speaking? In verse 14, the Lord identifies Himself as the "Amen," the "Faithful and True Witness," and the "Beginning of the creation of God." In other words, He is 100% trustworthy and He put a start to everything we see. As the "Amen," He is to be honored. As the "Faithful and True Witness," He is to be trusted. As the "Beginning of the creation of God," He is to be respected and His warning is to be feared. We'd be really stupid to not listen to someone with these credentials! Lord, help us to be wise!

What's the problem? Three times in verses 15 and 16 the Lord says they are neither "cold nor hot". He calls them lukewarm. In other words, they are not *passionate* like Him! Zeal or passion is an attribute of Christ, and if we are a proper reflection of Him, then it is an attribute of ours as well. Sometimes we think of zeal as an attribute of young Christians. We might hear God's people from time to time say things like, "Oh, he'll grow out of that." Well, fair enough if what we're talking about is an immature zeal or a self-driven zeal. But Christ-like zeal is an attribute of God *and* it is an attribute of sold-out, mature, Christ-honoring followers, too! If it's not an attribute of ours, then we are not like Christ and we must bow before the God of Zeal and repent of not reflecting Him properly!

Verse 17 reveals another major problem. They are not seeing the same way that He is seeing. They see themselves as rich, wealthy, and in need of nothing. He says that they are wretched, miserable, poor, blind, and naked. Again, wow! Christ communicates so well. We can get to seeing things a certain way, but what a wake-up call when the Lord shows us the reality of things from His perspective! The Laodiceans thought they were good to go – rich, wealthy, needing nothing (sound like the today's Church in North America?). The Lord Jesus steps in and says, "In reality you are wretched, miserable, poor, not wealthy. You can't see properly and your nakedness is on display." Wow, what a shocking evaluation.

How does Christ feel about it? In verse 16, the King of kings, Lord of lords, the high and lofty One who inhabits eternity, chooses a picturesque way of describing to us how He feels about lukewarmness among His followers. He says, in essence, it makes Him sick. *"I will vomit you out of my mouth,"* which literally means, to spew forth. How much clearer could Christ have been? 'I'm disgusted by this kind of Christian life,' He would say and then add: 'I'd rather you be totally cold and disinterested than lukewarm and maintaining the appearance of being Mine, but not being passionately sold out for My words, My example, My presence, My lifestyle.'

This is crazy shocking if we are thinking clearly. I'm amazed these days at how clearly our God communicates His heart and mind. I was in Kenya a few years ago with three other brothers teaching at elders' conferences. On a Saturday night I was feeling physically unsettled in my stomach. I woke on Sunday morning even more so. Later that day I was being driven to a hospital holding a bucket in my lap "spewing forth" violently. A month after returning home I had a relapse and once again was violently "vomiting" to the point that I had a seizure, passed out, and my poor wife had to figure out a way to get me to the doctor. That was a miserable sickness. It was an extremely unpleasant thing to go through multiple times, to say the least. (I feel badly to subject you to this story, but there is a meaningful purpose in doing so.)

It amazes me that this is how Christ chooses to communicate with us His feelings about lukewarmness. He would violently spew forth that type of Christianity. It also amazes me that I have a bride who loves me with a focused, dedicated, zealous love, and that He who is so *worthy*, so *glorious* so *all-consumingly awesome* does not. How can that be? Me, so unworthy and yet so blessed; He the focal point of the worship of Heaven and the cause of eternal delight, finds Himself in a place where He has to minister to and woo the Bride He has already purchased with His blood in order to get the love and zeal He so deserves. (see Hosea 2)

My brothers and sisters, these things ought not to be so. Will you pray with me that the Lord will so move and work in this generation that these things will not be so? Please, let us seek God about these things! Selah (pause and think about these things and, *"Seek the Lord and His power, seek His presence continually."* (Psalm 105:4)

His Advice: *"I counsel you to buy from Me"* (He's the source!)

- Refined gold – this would resolve their spiritual poverty. It's as if He is saying, 'I have all the wealth (spiritual resources) you'll ever need! Come and get it!'

- White garments – this would clothe them in practical holiness and cover their past shamefulness.

- Eye salve – this would provide them clear spiritual insight.

He says He wants them to have fine gold that they might "be rich;" garments that their current state might not be displayed to their shame, and He wants their eyes to be healed by the salve that He supplies so they can be a people of vision again! Wow, what a good heart the Lord has! How many of us would respond to a disinterested spouse by saying, "I'll be the solution to this whole problem that I didn't cause?" How many of us would be very tempted to be done with the miserable relationship? Not Christ! He accurately identifies where they are going wrong. He expresses clearly how He feels about it, and then He says, 'I'll fix the whole thing if you'll come to Me and get what I freely and lovingly offer you!' It reminds me so much of the call in Isaiah 55:1-3:

> "Ho! Everyone who thirsts, come to the waters; and you who have no money, come, buy and eat. Yes, come, buy wine and milk without money and without price. Why do you spend money for what is not bread, and your wages for what does not satisfy? Listen carefully to Me, and eat what is good, and let your soul delight itself in abundance. Incline your ear, and come to Me. Hear, and your soul shall live."

He reassures us of His love. Notice verse 19, *"As many as I love, I rebuke and chasten."* He might as well say, 'I'm talking to you this way so you'll get the message. I'm only talking to you this way because I love you, I long for you, I want things to be right badly enough, and I'm committed enough to this process that I'm rebuking you and chastening you so that you'll wake up and come back into the blessing of a proper relationship with Me.' Everyone is invited! Again, as it says in Isaiah 55, *"Everyone who thirsts, come!"*

What a heart our God has! How much grace, patience, love, and long-suffering go into the offers like this that we find scattered through the Word! Wow, praise God, Wow, thank You Lord, Wow!

His Summary. *"Be zealous and repent,"* verse 19. There is a lack of zeal among you; therefore be zealous! There is a lack of heat among you; therefore be hot! Being zealous/hot is the will of God. Being like Christ is the will of God for every child of God. This command is not recorded for super-Christians or elite soldiers. He is bidding everyone to come to Him, but many are ignoring His gentle voice.

There is no excuse for lukewarmness!

If we find ourselves in a lukewarm place it's our fault! (preaching at myself!) We must recognize the difference between the way we see ourselves and the way the Lord Jesus sees us, then repent (change our mind) and allow ourselves to be conformed to His will!

The Great Reward! *"Behold, I stand at the door and knock. If anyone* (emphasis mine) *hears My voice and opens the door, I will come in to Him and dine with him, and he with Me."* (Revelation 3:20) What is the *great reward* of repenting from lukewarmness? What is to be experienced by those who agree with God about how bad their life is, turn to God from their sin, and allow Him to create in them a Christ-like zeal once again? The answer is intimacy with Christ! Fellowship with Him! You get to enjoy Him in new ways that you've been missing out on! You get to walk with Him and talk with Him! You get a real, dynamic, living, breathing relationship with Christ that many or most in our North American Christianity have been missing out on or have theologically explained away as unbiblical! Please don't let it slip by that He says, *"I will come in to them and sup with them and they with Me."* Wow, that's an opportunity to fellowship with Christ, to walk with Him and talk with Him and to get to know Him better.

Christ is our great reward!

If this doesn't excite you then I don't know why you'd want to go to heaven. He is the focal point of heaven for all of eternity! Paul said, *"To live is Christ and to die is gain."* (Philippians 1:21) In other words, to live is Christ (now!) and to die is more of Christ! Absent from the body equals present with the Lord forever (see 2 Corinthians 5:8). Eternal life is to know Him (see John 17:3). Heaven is to be with Him!

If He is not enough to live for now, to die for now, to thrill your heart now as an all-consuming passion, why on earth would you want to go into an eternity where that all consuming passion not only exists but is focused and perfected in a never-ending eternal way, not to miss that He here mentions sitting with Him on His throne (an allusion to co-reigning. Wow again.)

His call is simple, straightforward, well communicated.

Who is speaking? The trustworthy One

What is the problem? You're not passionate the way you should be

How does Christ feel about it? It makes Him sick

His advice? Come get from Me all you need to solve this

His reassurance? Don't forget I love you more than you love yourself

His conclusion? Be zealous and repent

And the Reward? A real living breathing relationship with Christ (fellowship, communion, and reigning with Him)

The Lord Will Reward Your Zeal

Now, please notice in the context that not every Christian gets this! The ones who respond to His call, open the door, and are zealous and repent get what is described and the others miss out! This is so sobering, so serious!

I don't think it's a big leap for us to admit that lukewarmness characterizes the present condition of the Church in the North American. It's also not hard to understand Christ's solution for that issue. What may be difficult is truly agreeing with Christ and allowing painful biblical change to take place in our lives rather than making excuses or just putting it off. This is such a burden. Lord, help us. Lord, revive us. Right now, I cry out that we would be a people wholly for Him, aggressively and radically devoted.

We must be *passionate*, my friends! We must be zealous. If not, we're disgusting (vomitus) to the One who died for us. Lord, help us on for His glory! Lord, help us on into *all* that we have been given in Christ at salvation and *all* that He is waiting to bless us with, most of all Himself!

It is no marvel that the devil does not love field preaching! Neither do I; I love a commodious room, a soft cushion, a handsome pulpit. But where is my zeal if I do not trample all these underfoot in order to save one more soul?

Do all the good you can, in all the ways you can, to all the souls you can, in every place you can, at all the times you can, with all the zeal you can, as long as ever you can!

— John Wesley

We Must Have Power

Power: "Ability to do things, by virtue of strength, skill, resources, or authorization." (Tyndale Bible Dictionary)

Christ's Example of Power

Christ is our beautiful example here again. In Luke 3 the Lord is baptized by John. Some greatly used men of God of a previous generation would refer to this as "the baptism of power for service," as Christ was anointed by the Holy Spirit immediately after His baptism. In Acts 10:38, Peter refers to Christ's anointing by the Holy Spirit in this context, *"God anointed Jesus of Nazareth with the Holy Spirit and with power. He went about doing good and healing all who were oppressed by the devil, for God was with Him."* (Acts 10:38) Luke also informs us that the Lord Jesus was *"filled with the Spirit"* and *"led by the Spirit."* (Luke 4:1) Then, after forty days in the wilderness, Christ began His ministry in Galilee in the *"power* of the Spirit." Please notice the connection between the filling of the Spirit, the leading of the Spirit, and the *subsequent power* of the Spirit! There is an unmistakable connection in God's Word between the Spirit of God and *power!* There is an unmistakable connection between filling of the Spirit and *power!* There is an unmistakable connection in God's Word between the leading of the Spirit and *power!*

Jesus, as the perfect Man, (the God Man!) and as our perfect example, was filled with the Spirit. We are commanded in Ephesians 5:18 to, *"Be filled with the Spirit."* The Greek verb

59

literally means, 'be being filled' or in other words, 'be being constantly filled up to overflowing with the Spirit!' This is what it means to be "full of the Spirit." Christ lived this kind of life. Then through His apostle, Christ commands us to live ever-Spirit-filled lives.

Sometimes very well-meaning Christians get a bit gun shy when we start talking about the Spirit. Can I please say that all we should pursue is a Christlike life, and that is all we would ever encourage anyone to desire. He lived it. He commands us to live it. We do Him, the body of Christ, and ourselves, such a massive disservice when we pull back from what is Christlike and biblical in an effort not to be "too radical," or to "avoid pitfalls" that are seen in the world and the Church around us. We must embrace what Christ taught!

We must embrace all that Christ taught with
the full assurance that He would never lead us
into error, nor teach something that would
harm His people! We must follow Him forward!

The essential idea of the filling of the Spirit is not that you have more of the Spirit, but that the Spirit has more of you. The text says, *"Do not be drunk with wine,* (controlled by an outside force, in this case alcohol) *but be filled with the Spirit"* (controlled by an outside force, in this case the Spirit of God). (Ephesians 5:18) Both wine and the Holy Spirit can cause us to behave abnormally, but only what God stimulates in us pleases Him.

If we are filled with other things we can't be filled with the Spirit. If we are filled with a love for this world and the things in this world (e.g., 2 Tim. 4:10; 1 John 2:15-17); if we are filled with self, envy, bitterness, lust, etc.; then we miss the fullness of the Spirit-filled life that is commanded to be enjoyed. We must be emptied and yielded in order to be filled.

The hymn writer puts it so well:

> Emptied that Thou shouldest fill me,
> A clean vessel in Thy hand;
> With no power but as Thou givest,
> Graciously with each command.
> Channels only, blessed Master,
> But with all Thy wondrous power,
> Flowing through us, Thou canst use us,
> Every day and every hour.

> — Mary E. Maxwell

The Early Church's Example of Power

In Acts 1:8, the Lord Jesus told His disciples (now apostles), *"You shall receive **power** when the Holy Spirit has come upon you."* Where would the power come from? The Holy Spirit. When would the power come? When the Holy Spirit had come upon them. That's not very confusing, it is pretty simple to understand. The Holy Spirit's presence equals power.

In Acts 2, the Holy Spirit does indeed come as Christ had predicted (Pentecost). Timid, previously-denying Peter is turned into street-preaching, bold, effective Peter because he is now filled (controlled) by an outside force – the Spirit of God. 3,000 souls are saved that day (talk about power!) as a result of an empowered testimony.

It's interesting as you continue through the book of Acts that by Acts 4 there was a need to pray for boldness again in the face of persecution (v. 29). They prayed in a unified way, having set aside all covetousness, and the way the Lord answers their prayers is so instructive. He responds to their plea with the *"filling of the Holy Spirit"* and the overflow of that filling was the answer to their prayer for boldness (v. 31). As a result, the word of God went out by them with *"great power"* (v. 33). In other words, the answer to their prayer was the Holy Spirit filling them, *"such that great grace was upon them all"* (v. 33). The overflow of God's grace in them through the Holy Spirit produce the power and boldness that they knew they lacked in accomplishing what they knew God wanted them to do. This is so helpful and instructive.

This same spiritual power was evident in Stephen's life in Acts 6 and 7. Luke records, *"Stephen, full of faith and power, did great wonders and signs among the people. Then there arose some from what is called the Synagogue of the Freedmen (Cyrenians, Alexandrians, and those from Cilicia and Asia), disputing with Stephen. And they were not able to resist the wisdom and the Spirit by which he spoke."* (Acts 6:8-10) Stephen was full of power because his obedient faith permitted the Holy Spirit to have full control of him. This is why Luke says twice, that Stephen was *"full of the Holy Spirit"* (Acts 6:3, 7:55). Accordingly, in Acts 7 we witness Stephen boldly standing before and rebuking the entire Sanhedrin in the name of Jesus Christ. He preached boldly for Christ until the moment the enraged Jewish legalists stoned him dead. Stephen became the first martyr for Christ. He followed the example of His Spirit-led Savior in the ultimate display of spiritual power – personal sacrifice (see Hebrews 9:14).

Years later, Paul confirmed why the gospel had spread so powerfully across the Roman Empire, *"Because our gospel came to you not only in word, but also in power and in the Holy Spirit and with full conviction."* (1 Thessalonians 1:5) Only through the presence and power of the Holy Spirit could such a spectacular achievement have been accomplished.

Our Lack of Power

I have been focused on serving the Lord for thirty years now. I have given my life to this. I have labored to the point of exhaustion. Looking back, I really wonder how much of it was just me pursuing my vision and my goal of serving the Lord. How much of it was just me trying to do something for God? How much was me being in control, as opposed to the Holy Spirit? How much was Scott's effort, as opposed to Christ working through me? The answer is clearly, "I don't know." I think the Lord in His grace will likely never show me. At the Judgment Seat, Christ will burn up the things done in the flesh and no one will be happier than me to see all that go. (I should say here that I commend hard work for the Lord! God's Word says repeatedly things like be steadfast, immoveable abounding in the work of the Lord! I'm definitely not arguing against hard work! But I'm totally arguing against hard work done by human effort as opposed to the way the Scripture says it should be done, i.e., filled with the Spirit, being led by and empowered by the Spirit, walking in the Spirit. In other words: Christ doing His work through us!)

For the better part of twenty years of adult ministry, I have been part of quiet conversations with admirable servants of God who ask things like, "Why the lack of power?" and, "Why the lack of fruitfulness?" I can remember when, after years of noticing the downward trend among many of God's people, I asked a friend if the Church in North America was declining, and without hesitation he told me that it was. I remember being so troubled but without any real answers and I began to seek the Lord about these things. Well, the Lord has taught many things since then and this is definitely one of the most important.

Being filled by the Holy Spirit equates to New Testament POWER. A lack of power can be traced back to resisting, grieving and quenching the Holy Spirit of God.

Fruitlessness is strongly rebuked in God's Word, but fruitfulness is assured if we abide in Christ (see John 15:2, 5).

Why do we lack New Testament *power?* If we take the time to go back and read the Scripture asking why, the answer seems to come rather quickly and simply. Power is associated with the Holy Spirit. We live in the age of the Spirit, the Church Age. If we live our lives as the Word describes, there will be evidence of the Holy Spirit's power. If we do not, no amount of planning or money or effort or correct-but-dead orthodoxy can substitute for *the power* that comes when He is free to fill, control, move, and guide. We cannot do this on our own. We must, *must* seek the Lord and submit to His way, the way we always should have done but sadly not the way we always have.

What kind of life do we want to live? I can't stand the idea of living the Christian life the way I did before. I'd rather die than go back to trying to do something for God, rather than abiding and seeing Him work through me.

The Empowered Life

The Scripture describes the empowered-life that all believers are to enjoy:

Empowered prayer: *"Confess your trespasses to one another, and pray for one another, that you may be healed. The effective (energeo), fervent prayer of a* *righteous man avails much."* (*Energeo*: activated, full of power in order to achieve results.) James 5:16

Empowered testimony: *"That the sharing of your faith may become effective (energes) by the acknowledgement of every good thing which is in you in Christ Jesus."* (*Energes* -same root as *energeo*) Philemon 6

Empowered working: *"For He who worked effectively (energeo) in Peter for the apostleship to the circumcised also worked effectively (energeo) in me toward the Gentiles."* Galatians 2:8

"For it is God who works in you both to will and to do for His good pleasure." Philippians 2:13

"To this end I also labor, striving according to His working which works in me mightily." Colossians 1:29

Empowered open doors: *"For a great and effective (energes) door has opened to me, and there are many adversaries."* 1 Corinthians 16:9

The Greek words *energeo* and *energes* found in the above verses can be rendered "to energize" or "energized" for work, respectively. This is the only way to live – energized by God! This is certainly the only way I want to live! Lord, help us by grace alone to be conformed to His Word and His way and to come into all He has for us for His glory and our good!

Where Do We Go From Here?

We must take a serious look at ourselves in the mirror of God's Word and we must not go away forgetting what we see. We must look at the powerlessness among us, the evidence of fleshly living in our local churches, and realize that we are not where we are by divine decree, but by human failing. We have allowed ourselves to slide away from biblical Christianity in preference to North American Christianity. We must recognize that this is evil in God's sight and we cannot go on this way.

Confess and Forsake

God is a God of love and compassion and longsuffering. There is really no question that He will forgive but we must first come to Him in honesty and humility confessing our wrong. *"He who covers his sins will not prosper, but whoever confesses and forsakes them will have mercy."* (Proverbs 28:13)

Draw Near

We find this crazy awesome promise in James 4:8, *"Draw near to God and He will draw near to you."* This is backed up by Psalm 145:18, *"The Lord is near to all those who call upon Him, to those who call upon Him in truth."* It is truly amazing grace that the Lord commits Himself to us in this way. He guarantees that if we come back to Him, He will come back to us, and the power that we lack, that we long for, isn't actually the primary goal – it is an overflow of a proper relationship with Christ!

Pray

In Luke 11:13, the Lord Jesus instructs His followers to pray for the Holy Spirit. *"How much more will your Heavenly Father give the Holy Spirit to those who ask?"* We don't believe for our day that this means the indwelling of the Holy Spirit or the baptism of the Holy Spirit or the sealing of the Holy Spirit. But if you carefully work through this text it becomes evident that the Lord Jesus here is referring to the effects of having the Holy Spirit, the ministries of the Spirit – power, joy, intimacy, leading, filling, and anointing.

"It is significant that the gift He selects as the one we most need, and the one He most desires to give, is the Holy Spirit."
— J. G. Bellet

When Jesus spoke these words, the Holy Spirit had not yet been given (John 7:39). Today we should not pray for the Holy Spirit to be *given* to us as an indwelling Person, because He comes to indwell us at the time of our conversion (Romans 8:9b; Ephesians 1:13-14). It is certainly proper and necessary for us to pray for the Holy Spirit in other ways. We should pray that we will be teachable by the Holy Spirit, that we will be guided by the Spirit, and that His power will be poured out on us in all our service for Christ.

The Greek text of Luke 11:13 informs us that God wants believers to take full advantage of His goodness so that they can be fully equipped for service in an ongoing way:

In the original Greek, verse 13 does not say that God will give *the* Holy Spirit, but rather He will "give Holy Spirit" (without the article). Professor H. B. Swete pointed out that when the article is present, it refers to the Person Himself, but when the article is absent, it refers to His gifts or operations on our behalf. So, in this passage, it is not so much a prayer for the *Person* of the Holy Spirit, but rather for His ministries in our lives. This is further borne out by the parallel passage in Matthew 7:11 which reads, *"… how much more will your Father who is in heaven give good things to those who ask Him!"*[3]

It is quite possible that when the Lord taught the disciples to ask for *the Holy Spirit*, He was referring to the *power* of the

Spirit that would enable them to live the otherworldly type of discipleship that He had been teaching in the preceding chapters. By this time, they were probably feeling how utterly impossible it was for them to meet the tests of discipleship in their own strength. This is, of course, true. *The Holy Spirit* is the power that enables us to live the Christian life. So the Lord noted that His Father yearned to give this power to those who ask.

Yield and Obey

The instruction in Ephesians 5 says, "Be filled," not strive to be filled. When we rightly discern what Scripture is saying, we understand this relates to us yielding to God. It's His will for us. If we are properly emptied and yielded and given over to Him wholly (Romans 12:1-2), then we will be filled and the New Testament life, power, joy, and eternal focus, will all flow out of us. Christ's life within us, must be lived out the way Christ intended!

Years ago I started praying for a desperately needed revival. When I say praying, I mean a daily commitment to pray with likeminded brothers for this. I remember day after day of excruciating labor in prayer. I remember saying to the Lord that I didn't know how long I could keep this up, feeling a heaviness after each morning's prayer session as if I had attended the funeral of a dearly loved one. I remember when the Lord showed me that my prayers were slightly off. That I shouldn't *primarily* seek a by-product of Christ (in this case revival), but rather I should *primarily* be seeking Christ Himself, and that all else that I longed for would flow from Him! "Seek the Lord and His *power*, seek His presence continually." (Psalm 105:4) Well, we see a very similar thing here. *Power* is the by-product of a proper Biblically functioning relationship with the Lord. We don't need to seek power primarily. We need to wholly seek *Him* with all our heart, be given over to *Him* day by day. We can believe *Him* to give us all the power that we will ever need for *His* glory and *His* purposes to be realized in and through us.

If I get to the end of my life and hear others speaking of my abilities and accomplishments, I will consider my life a horrible failure.

I would weep and weep at that moment, and I'm frankly terrified of that thought. We must live a life characterized by the power of God that can only be explained by His might so all looking on will say, "Look what God has done!"

Lord, help us. *"Not by might nor by power but by my Spirit sayeth the Lord."* (Zechariah 4:6)

Just as water ever seeks and fills the lowest place, so the moment God finds you abased and empty, His glory and power flow in.

— Andrew Murray

We Must Pursue

"If anyone comes to Me and does not hate his father and mother, wife and children, brothers and sisters, yes and his own life also, he cannot be my disciple." Luke 14:26

"Whoever does not bear his cross and come after Me cannot be My disciple. For which of you, intending to build a tower, does not sit down first and count the cost?" Luke 14:27-28

"So likewise, whoever of you does not forsake all that he has cannot be My disciple." Luke 14:33

Forsake to Follow

What are we honestly willing to give up for Christ? What are we willing to sacrifice to see Christ's great agenda accomplished through us in our generation? Will we give up comfort? Career goals? Living near dearly loved family? Our own dreams of what we hoped life would be? Would we trade our hopes and dreams and aspirations for a cross of suffering, a cross that the world would mock, and many Christians would misunderstand?

The real biblical question is not would we give up just something, but would we give up *everything*? I pray right now the words of the Lord Jesus will deeply impact those of you reading this.

"Whoever of you does not forsake all that he has cannot be My disciple." Luke 14:33

Wow, what a standard and what a requirement! Death to self, ambition, comfort, and any sense of earthly gain. (The world is crucified to me and I to the world. Gal. 6:14)

This is the call of Christ and His warning looms large: *"He who finds his life will lose it, and he who loses his life for My sake will find it."* (Matthew 10:39) We're on the last chapter of the message the Lord gave me, and I suppose it's time we paused to take stock again. Are you willing to go forward with Christ? Are you willing to forsake all? Let me encourage you and warn you, He will take you at your word. God's Word warns against rash or thoughtless vows to the Lord. I encourage each of us to think this through. And yes, I believe 100 percent what Christ said, that if you lose your life for His sake then you'll find it, and that this is the only life worth living. I also know that death to self feels like dying. It involves a journey of many tears and much Christ-like suffering but let me please say again that what it gives birth to is mind-blowingly awesome. It's such a rich quality of life with Him that you'd rather die than go back. In fact, there is really no going back no matter what lies ahead.

So, my friend, please think this through and simply bow your head and "commit" yourself to Christ for the first time or once again. This word "commit" is a beautiful word in Scripture. It means to hand oneself over to someone to keep, use, take care of, or manage any way that that person sees fit. In 1 Peter 2:23, Christ does this and hands Himself over to the Father. In the same book we are urged to follow His example of doing so. Please, my precious brothers and sisters, don't live your Christian life and miss out on the whole point of it –

intimacy with Christ! Please don't hit the lottery in coming to know Christ then decide you're happy living on $30,000 a year spiritually when all the riches are at your disposal, the greatest of which by far is a real, tangible, practical, love relationship with Jesus Himself!

I start the chapter this way because we are going to discuss pursuing Christ's great agenda in our day and following Him forward in His desire to see this generation reached with His "good news" (gospel). If we're not truly disciples, we're choosing a life of powerlessness, compromise, guilt, and distance rather than intimacy. We can't accomplish His great agenda without Him! We must be all in, and then we must follow Him and let Him "make us fishers of men".

That is one of the most encouraging phrases in Scripture for me when it comes to this subject of pursuing the lost. *"Follow Me and I will make you fishers of men."* (Matthew 4:19) I consider myself one of the worst evangelists in North America. I can be crazy awkward (and frequently am crazy awkward) in gospel situations. We just had a 'coffee with a cop' time in our community. My wife and I put together little thank you gift packets for the officers and as we drove close to the event, man I got nervous. My wife actually said to me, "Do you want me to do it?" and I said a quick no, not wanting to chicken out or fail the Lord. I walked up to the officers holding my little packets and I just didn't know how to transition. I talked with them, thanked them for their service, chatted, and then walked away back to where my wife was ordering coffee for us. She looked at me and said, "It would be less awkward if you gave them the gift the first time," and I said, "I know."

Eventually the Lord did help me figure out my transition and how to offer them the gift that we had for them. Each officer accepted. Some very gratefully accepted and appreciated what we were doing for them. My point is that I don't want to give the impression that I'm a super Christian who has figured out this whole life and service thing, and that boldness and Christlike tact in the gospel isn't something I'm not constantly dependent on Him for. That would be such a sin if I came across that way. "Follow Me and I will make you," – that's my hope, that's my promise. I love watching the Lord working in me, the biggest chicken of all, the most awkward of all, but I know God's will for me is to be a light and an empowered testimony. And so, I precede based on faith in His promises that His will is to use me and to have me shine.

For the Lord's glory, I want to also share with you about how not long ago in our community, I was driving along with my wife and we saw a young teenage drug addict named Chris (not his real name). He was walking along Main Street bawling when we drove by. I saw him and immediately said to my wife, "Pull over!" She did, so I grabbed a couple pieces of the gospel literature I had in our vehicle and jumped out. I started walking after him as quickly as I was able, and as soon as I was within ear shot of him, I started calling his name. I couldn't help myself frankly. The burden of his lost and suffering soul was more than I could take.

He was walking away from me saying, "I want my mom!"

I was crying out after him saying, "Jesus loves you more than you can imagine!" "You don't have to live like this." "Christ will set you free." "God so loved the world He gave His only Son!"

He started saying, "Why are you following me?"

I kept responding, "You need Christ!"

Eventually, I did catch him, and he turned and looked at me. He is built like a bull and could crush me I'm sure. He looked at me, scared and defensive, and said one more time, "What do you want?" I just calmly, without giving it any thought at all said, "I just want to give you this piece of paper that talks about Jesus Christ from the Bible and I want you to hear that He loves you and would so gladly set you free from the misery and destruction of sin." (see Romans 6:13-18) He said, "Set it down". I set it in the grass. He stepped forward to pick it up and crying he went on his way.

My point is simple. I want to be completely open and forthright with you about my limitations and the things I am constantly cast upon the Lord for, and I also want to be open and forthright with you about how real the Lord's help is when we "follow Him" and He "makes us fishers of men".

He will do this. It's a promise you can claim and cling to. It all starts with a proper love relationship with Him.

He meets you where you are and moves you
piece by piece to be like Him.

Three Lost Things

Luke 15 displays the Lord Jesus' heart in a remarkable way. At the beginning of the chapter four kinds of people are coming near Him but not all for the same purpose. Tax collectors and sinners are drawing near to "hear Him" (v. 1). Pharisees and Scribes come near to complain and find fault with Him (v. 2). He responds to this complex situation by telling a story, one story with three parts, and if we take time to enter into what He's doing and saying here, we see an answer to the Pharisees and Scribes' criticism that is beautiful and inspiring, and life changing. The Pharisees and Scribes say, "This Man receives sinners and eats with them. So Christ spoke this parable to them, saying...."

He then tells a story about three lost things: a lost sheep, a lost coin, and a lost son (though both sons were actually lost). Please remember that He is answering an objection made by the religiously minded people of the day. They said things like, "Why is this man spending time with people like that?" "We are the respectable people around here and we would never do that!" Christ's answer was really life changing for me when I saw it years ago. He basically says, through a brilliant 3-fold story, "If you look around, you'll see people who are *helplessly* lost (sheep), you'll see people who are *unconsciously* lost (coin), and you'll see people that are *willfully* lost (prodigal son). And let Me show you how people like yourselves are religiously lost (Scribes and Pharisees who end up outside the door at the end of the story, missing out on the fellowship the Father desires to have with them)".

Please pause now and go and read Luke 15. I encourage you to read it slowly, thoughtfully, maybe even multiple times if that would help it sink into your heart and mind.

Okay, you're back! Let's pull this chapter apart a bit and see how Christ thinks and how He views pursuing the souls that He loves so deeply.

The Lost Sheep

The first part of the Lord's story describes a lost sheep – the helplessly lost sinner. The sheep has no great defense mechanism, no big teeth, no great military mind, no wings to fly away. Its safety is totally found in how close it finds itself to the shepherd. When it's lost, it is in terrible danger. It can fall prey to cold weather, to pits, to predators that would rip it in pieces and devour it. The Lord looks at a whole category of people this way; they are helplessly lost. He sees them suffering, being used and abused, consumed by others, chewed up and spit out, and His heart of love can't stand to leave them in that state. So in Luke 15 He's spending time with them. When the religiously minded people object, He basically says, "Look at them, look at how helpless and needy they are. These are the ones I came to look for! Of course, I'm spending time with them! I love them and long for them to come to Me that they might be safe and have true eternal life!"

How beautiful is Christ's heart! How worship-worthy is the Savior's mindset!

The Son of God made the trip from the glories of Heaven to a sin cursed earth, where He would be misunderstood, mocked, rejected, questioned; where He would bear the sins of the *entire world,* experience a separation in fellowship with the Father as He became sin on our behalf, every step of the way displaying the heart of love His Father has? Wow! Praise God and thank You, Lord, for the heart You have toward people like me, helplessly lost sinners, now wonderfully found by grace through faith and safe and happy in Your arms forever.

Have you ever known someone who was a sinner like that, a helplessly lost sinner? There are countless millions of them. It brings me to tears to think of them, out there in the world suffering and being abused. You can kind of understand why Christ wept over Jerusalem multiple times and said, "I would have gathered you as a hen gathers her chicks but you would not," and here you can begin to feel Christ's heart when He speaks, "...you would not come to Me that you might have life." (John 5:40)

There was a girl Lynn and I tried to work with years ago. She came from a miserable background and left the home she grew up in as soon as she turned 18. Out on her own and obviously a helplessly lost sheep, I remember observing with my wife, 'That girl is going to be snatched up, and used and abused by whoever first shows any interest in her.' One day as she reached for something, when the sleeve of her shirt pulled up her arm, we noticed that she had been cutting herself – a silent cry of desperation and an attempt at dealing with pain.

As we tried to help her, she told us that as she had come out of a store a number of nights before, a man had shown interest in her. She had ended up spending the night with him. She was hurt when he didn't call after that and his interest was gone. The same thing happened again shortly later. All the while my wife and I were trying to share Christ with her and lead her to the Man who would truly selflessly love, protect and satisfy her, but things just seemed to get worse and worse for her as she wandered around the wilderness of life being used and abused. Eventually she came by to say goodbye. She had a rough, gross, vulgar looking man with her who looked to be three times her age. She announced to us that they were going to get married. She then grabbed a few things, and off they went. We've never seen her again. I wonder as I write this where she is, how her life has gone. I'm glad that she is not beyond Christ's loving reach if she is still alive. I pray for her to find Christ before it's too late.

A dear friend of mine who is giving his life for the gospel told me a number of months ago that there are 348 unreached people groups in the United States and Canada. Is that shocking to you? Man, it was to me! If someone had asked me how many unreached people groups from around the world could be found in the US and Canada, I'm sure I'd have guessed 25 maybe, but 348, wow! One of these people groups lives in the backyard of the community where my wife Lynn and I live now. These are people coming from unreached people groups around the world, whom the Lord in His loving sovereignty has brought here to North America! We don't even have to go around the world to find them. We just have to be willing to uproot and move on this continent, in our own culture, or look and see who is in our backyard and be willing to do the work of reaching them with the truth of Christ! Talk about an open door, wow, and Lord, help us.

There are so many helplessly lost sheep. So many used and abused that Christ's heart longs for and that we are tasked with finding and loving on His behalf.

Please Lord, help us for Your glory, help us move forward for the salvation of the helplessly lost. Change us and make us those who just can't stand to not be out there looking and loving and sharing.

The Lost Coin

The second part of the story describes a lost coin. This is a great picture of an unconsciously lost sinner. The coin is just sitting there. It's not worried or anxious, and it doesn't know that it's lost or that it needs to be found. It doesn't realize how much it is treasured by its owner. It's not where it ought to be, in the place of safety with the other nine coins. It's unable to look for the owner. It's just sitting there and needs someone to go and look for it. Wow, there are so many parallels to be seen between this coin and a huge category of sinners that Christ desires to be reached on His behalf.

"How will they hear without a preacher?" (Romans 10:14) *"Faith comes by hearing and hearing by the word of God."* (Romans 10:17)

I was recently tasked with preaching at a conference on Philippians 1. As I prepared, the biggest thing that stood out to me was the emphasis on the gospel. Fellowship of the gospel (v. 5), completion of the gospel (my title; v. 6), defense and confirmation of the gospel (v. 7; also v. 17), furtherance of the gospel (v. 12), preach Christ (twice in vv. 15-16), Christ is preached (v. 18), and having conduct worthy of the gospel and striving together for the gospel (v. 27). Any way in which Christ is preached brings Paul to rejoicing including less than righteous motivations (vv. 15-18)!

79

If we understand what Paul is saying at all, we understand that Christ must be preached! There are over 575 million souls on this great continent and a vast many of them are just like that coin! They don't know they're lost. They don't know the eternal danger they are in. *"It is appointed unto man once to die, then comes the judgment."* Hebrews 9:27

They have no concept that they are one breath or one heartbeat away from a lost eternity where the chance of salvation would then be behind them!

Christ did an amazing job of being the Light of the World. Now He is seated at the right hand of the Father and it's our job to "Go into the world and preach the gospel to every creature." Gospel work is just that, *work*. It must be done. The work must be done in our day by people who are willing to live for Christ's agenda rather than for their own. It must be done by little, needy, incapable servants who are willing to follow Christ and let Him "make them" fishers of men.

In essence Christ is saying, 'I came to reach people just like this. Look at them. A whole category of them have no idea they're lost and I'm here to tell them. They'll choose how they respond, and my job is to love them and tell them.' *"The Spirit of the Lord is upon Me, because He has anointed Me to preach the gospel to the poor; He has sent Me to heal the brokenhearted, to proclaim liberty to the captives and recovery of sight to the blind, to set at liberty those who are oppressed."* (Luke 4:18)

The Lost Son (The Prodigal Son)

After talking about the helplessly lost sheep, and the unconsciously lost coin, the Lord now brings up the third precious category of souls that He longs for, that He is happy to spend time with, the prodigals. These are the party animals. These are the willfully lost sinners. They know they're lost, and they delight in it. They're the ones who, at their doors, will tell you they'd go to Hell if they died today, and many of them have believed the lie from the pit of Hell that they'd rather party in Hell with the devil than go to Heaven. They don't know the biblical concept of Hell, that Satan, and the demons are going to be eternally tormented in conscious punishment (see Revelation 20:10), as will those who reject God's offer of salvation through Jesus Christ in this life. These are the Las Vegas loving sinners.

If you have any question of what I mean, read the portion of the story again. (Luke 15:11-32) You'll see a boy who wanted the benefits of his father (give me my inheritance) but not intimacy with his father (I'll go to a far-off land). You'll see a boy who wasted his father's hard-worked-for-inheritance on partying or "prodigal living' (v. 13) and prostitutes or "harlots" (v. 30).

Let's pause to notice here that there is no question that what this boy did was disgraceful. There is no excuse for it. But the father's love for his son shines even more beautifully through the misery of his sin and debauchery.

The father loves his son, the father longs for his son's return. He longs to forgive and receive back. This is the heart of God.

81

That's the heart that looked for me. That's the heart that ran to me when I came back and admitted my sin. Wow, thank and praise and worship the God who has such a heart and displays it perfectly in His Word, and constantly through His actions in the world around us.

Do you know any willfully lost sinners? Any party animals out there who refuse to see the truth because they know if they acknowledged it then they would have to change their lifestyle and they're not willing to come to Christ that they might have life?

I've heard so many people say they want to repent later; they want to enjoy life now. They don't totally reject the truth of Christ's claims, but they are unwilling to turn to Him from their sin (repent) and accept His free gift of eternal life (volitional belief). I love the way John 1:12 says it, "But as many as *received* (volitional faith) Him, to them He gave the right to become children of God, to those who *believe* (volitional faith) in His name." (volitional: relating to the use of one's will)

This kind of thinking is so stupid and misguided, when you think of what's at stake, when you realize that so many of those who plan to repent at 11:59 when their day/life is far spent, and then they die at 11:30 and their chance at salvation is gone; when you realize that Christ is real life (see 1 Timothy 6:12, 19) and that He is the mind-blowing fulfillment of everything that truly satisfies and is the only thing that will fill up the longing of the human heart. Lord, help us to represent Him the way He deserves to a lost and desperately needy world, that He might be lifted up in practical ways and sinners will be drawn to Him!

Will you go?

Christians agree that Christ has commanded us to go. Really, practically, this is not disputable. People who genuinely disagree on the subject of Calvinistic and Arminian thought (or reject both as extreme) totally agree on two wonderful points that should unite us under Christ's banner and help us forward with Him! 1) No one would be saved without God's pre-salvific work, and 2) Christ must be preached!

Can we embrace these two points and move forward in utter dependence and humility but with fierce passion and confidence in Him?

Some would rather sit around and argue fine theological points than go forward under Christ's banner. I feel sorry for these Christians, missing out on so much now and in eternity. I would never minimize the Lord's instruction to rightly divide the Word of Truth, never minimize or trivialize the massive importance of proper Christ honoring doctrine, but if it becomes the entire end-goal to the point that we are not obeying it and living it, then that is dead orthodoxy, an issue which is seriously harming the Church in North America.

Some are so burdened down by 'rubbish' and they legitimately don't have time with their current lifestyle to have Christ's priorities as their priorities. If this is you, will you see that the way you've ordered your life (although normal in North American Christianity) is evil and a form of rebellion in the presence of God, and will you let Him lead you to repentance, to biblical change, to the freeing up of your life so it can be spent on His agenda rather than wasted on your presuppositions of what a normal Christian life is to look like?

Some are afraid (like me perhaps) of messing it up or representing Christ poorly so that they accept a compromised and powerless life. Rather, we should let the Lord change our view; from looking at ourselves, (and hence defeat) to looking at Him. We should trust and believe in Him, having confidence in Him and His ability to use us rather than in our ability to be skillful. We must let Him lead us into fruitfulness, where so much powerlessness and fruitlessness has remained for too long.

Go Forward

I say let's follow Christ forward in His obvious and clearly stated agenda for our day. He is the Lord of the harvest! He has always done His job well. He is not discouraged and will not fail (Isaiah 42:4).

You don't have to make yourself be something. You don't have to win the battle. All of that has been done for you. You just simply have to forsake all and follow. Be filled, be yielded, daily die to self and live for Christ and what He leads us into will blow our minds. It's eternal life now!

I have a precious daughter named Rebekah. She is such a treasure to me. She is beautiful and delightful like her mom. When I think of the way the Lord loves the world these days, I think of her. If some evil man had her, if he was carrying her away to unimaginable and unspeakable treatment, if she had terror in her eyes and was crying out looking to anyone for help, if I could see her but somehow, I couldn't get to her and I cried to you to go and save her but you wouldn't do it, how would you expect me to respond? How would you expect me to feel at your unwillingness to do anything and everything within your power to see my precious girl saved from things that aren't even worthy of words because they are so awful?

What if you responded to my call by telling me you were scared?

What if you told me you were too busy, that you'd want to do it but don't have the time?

What if you'd rather sit around debating the theological points of the matter rather than reaching out your hand to actually rescue someone from unimaginable horror?

How would you want me to respond? Oh, that's OK. I understand. It's hard. I know you're very busy. Would any response other than you doing everything in your power at that moment to save her be acceptable? NO! My father's heart would demand that you do all you could, perhaps even lay down your life to rescue my precious girl.

How can we think of God's love any less than my love? How can we think of our obligation to Him as any less than the obligation to me in the scenario presented?

The problem is that I don't love souls around me to the same extent that I love my Rebekah. Too often, (most often!) I don't feel about them the same way Christ feels about them. We must live a life of intimacy with Christ and let the love of God be poured into our hearts (Romans 5:5) to such an extent that we do begin to feel what He feels for them, so we can't help ourselves but share. When we are so in love with Him and so filled up with love for Him it will be natural for Him to come out in what we say from day to day. Light shines. It doesn't try to shine, it just shines. When it is properly cultivated and healthy, it just shines in the darkness.

Christ gave His life for us. We now have the joy and eternal privilege of giving our lives for Him! Lord, help us.

No one can sum up all God is able to accomplish through one solitary life, wholly yielded, adjusted, and obedient to Him.

— D. L. Moody

We Must Be Purposeful

The Conclusion

If we are not pure, then by definition we are resisting, grieving, and quenching the Holy Spirit. Rather than seeing Christ exalted and His omnipotent power flowing through us, we will see failure, frustration, and compromise.

If we are not prayerful, then we are refusing to submit to and obey so many vital exhortations in God's Word. How can we expect to go forward with Christ if we are refusing His Lordship in our lives now? Faithful in little, faithful in much!

If we are not passionate, we are living a type of Christian life that is disgusting (vomitus) to our Leader. Lukewarmness shows us where our heart truly is. Even a football team expects more from its participants than lukewarmness.

If we have no omnipotent power evident in our lives and ministries, how could we ever expect to see the Church revived and the lost reached?

If we will not pursue the lost who are deeply loved by Christ, if we will not allow Him to so saturate our lives that His love becomes our love and His voice becomes our voice and His hands become our hands to reach out, then we're not really functioning as a part of His great agenda.

In the end, the argument is so simple. Christ is the Way, the Truth, and the Life. He is the way forward. Intimacy with Him and a proper abiding love relationship with Him (John 15:9-16, Jude 20-21) overflows in purity, prayer, passion, power and pursuing.

Purity – holiness is the overflow of a love relationship with Christ

Prayer – prayer is the expression of a love relationship with Christ

Passion – Zeal/passion is the outcome of a proper intimate love relationship with Christ

Power – the Lord is looking for those who will be wholly yielded in their love relationship and hence filled, displaying His power to save, sanctify, revive, and change.

Pursuit – a heart filled to overflowing with Christ's love is going to be a heart that can't help but love those around it, seeking their best, and sharing the truth of eternal life with them.

It really all flows from Him. Praise God! He is the answer to every need. He is the One who is wise enough to navigate every pitfall.

We become either the generation that we read about in Jeremiah that went back and not forward by refusing intimacy and yieldedness, (Jeremiah 7:24) or we go forward to victory in our day through yieldedness, filling, faithfulness in whatever is set before us now, and letting Him lead and grow us in a never-ending way, all the way home to eternity with Him.

I don't really care if the Lord uses this little book or if He chooses to use something far better, but I sit here burdened to tears for this generation of North American Christians. I hunger and ache with all my heart and soul and mind and strength for us not to be a generation that wanders around in the wilderness and dies (spiritually) because of any evil and ugly form of unbelief and unyieldedness. We must rather be a generation that wholly follows the Lord into His victories, into the practical displays of His glory that He is so worthy of, and into the eternal joy of His presence with the satisfaction of having given all for the One who gave His all for us.

My brothers and sisters let us **GO FORWARD** with Christ and never go back.

I am prepared to go anywhere, so long as it is **forward**.

— David Livingstone

Endnotes

[1]   William MacDonald, *Believer's Bible Commentary* (Thomas Nelson Publishers, Nashville, TN; 1989), p. 1931

[2]   Ibid.

[3]   Ibid., p. 1413

Lightning Source UK Ltd.
Milton Keynes UK
UKHW020719220621
385948UK00007B/984